WALKING THE LONDON BLITZ

WALKING THE LONDON BLITZ

Clive Harris

Leo Cooper

First published in 2003 and reprinted in 2011 by
LEO COOPER
an imprint of
Pen & Sword Books Limited
47 Church Street, Barnsley, South Yorkshire S70 2AS

ISBN 1 84415 960 3

A CIP catalogue of this book is available
from the British Library

Printed by CPI UK

For up-to-date information on other titles produced under the Leo Cooper
imprint, please telephone
or write to:

Pen & Sword Books Ltd, FREEPOST, 47 Church Street
Barnsley, South Yorkshire S70 2BR
Telephone 01226 734222

Contents

PREFACE

My earliest childhood memory is of the sitting room of our terraced house in Knella Road, Welwyn Garden City, in 1971. My dad lifts me up on his shoulders to look at a row of rusty curtain hooks attached to which are the remnants of a dark heavy fabric. 'These were blackout curtains from the war. Remember them, as they have to come down now.' He was decorating. An afternoon visit followed to an air raid siren on a telegraph pole in a nearby street. Thus, in a working class suburb of a town just twenty miles from the centre of London, my lifelong fascination with history began.

More recently I have studied, researched and guided groups around the many battlefields of the Great War along with my friend and fellow author Paul Reed. Paul lives with his family in the village of Courcelette on the Somme. Working alongside him on tours has led to people often asking, 'Wouldn't you like to live on a battlefield?' More recently I have taken to pointing out that I do. For just as the Battle of Waterloo was reputedly won on the playing fields of Eton, Britain, alone, stood firm against the might of Hitler's Luftwaffe and did so in my backyard.

The generation that fought in the Great War, some of whom I have had the privilege to meet, also have their role to play in this story, for, more often than not, alongside their Great War medals, the orange and green ribbon of the Defence Medal can also be found. These men, after fighting the war to end all wars, returned home to find themselves once again in the front line twenty years later. This time they filled the ranks of the auxiliary and national fire services, police officers, ambulance drivers, ARP wardens, rescue workers, fire-watchers and the myriad other roles that made up

An A.F.S. volunteer, like many of his colleagues a Great War veteran.

London's civil defence during the Blitz.

There are many works on the Blitz already available and this book does not seek to replace them. Instead it is a handy pocket guide to events that occurred in and around the City during the war. My mother's family came from Acton, W3. However, due to self-imposed restrictions, their experiences are not included. Likewise, heavily populated areas such as the East End or South London are missing from these pages, but have not been omitted through lack of respect or knowledge. Their story deserves its own book.

What this book does offer is the chance to see our city's last remaining 'rusty curtain hooks' before they are all taken down. In a series of walks we are able to rediscover London's more recent history by way of monuments that record brave deeds and spots where similar feats are long since forgotten. We visit museums dedicated to the city in war and look at the 'honourable scars' that remain on buildings.

My thanks must go to my parents Lyn and Brian Harris for lifting me up all those summers ago; my soulmate Ali who has supported me and grown up with me for the last 18 years and who this year gave me the honour of becoming my wife; Nicola and Margaret for providing support and guidance in life as and when I require it, my mate John Mogie, who walked the walks with me and proved himself as my best friend and best man. I am also very fortunate in having two good friends in Paul Reed and Kieron Hoyle who have given me the confidence to write a book of my

A typical London street pre-war. Stirling Road, Acton, including the author's grandparents, celebrate the Silver Jubilee of 1935.

The 'honourable scars' on London's buildings remain visible to this day.

own and finally to my grandfather L/AC Frank Harris, 19SQN, Royal Air Force, who, like his generation, was prepared to give his tomorrow for our today.

The view from my bedroom window in the peaceful Hertfordshire village of Woolmer Green overlooks fields and farmland and a small copse nestles in a large hollow to the frustration of the farmer who has to plough around it every year. The field has been ploughed in this manner for the last 58 years for its marks the spot where the last V1 'doodlebug' fired on London landed harmlessly and somewhat ironically in a sewage pit that once existed there. Time has indeed moved on and the tangible evidence of the last war is fading, as are the ranks of people who played their part in it. For their memory and for whatever your own reasons I hope you gain as much from walking these routes as I did researching them.

At certain spots, such as Birdcage Walk or Stainer Street, I found an overwhelming feeling of sadness, at others, such as St Paul's or Covent Garden, I found hope. There were busy non-stop areas like Leadenhall Street with its city workers and quiet reflective places like St Olave's in Hart Street with its shade and peace, but wherever I was if I stopped and listened I could have sworn that, in the distance, a nightingale still sang in Berkeley Square.

Clive Harris, Twin Foxes, 2002

ACKNOWLEDGEMENTS

Apart from those mentioned above, there are a number of friends, colleagues and contributors without whom this book would not have been possible. Whilst it in not feasible to include all of them, I would like to thank the following: my editor Tom Hartman for all his guidance and support, the staff at Pen & Sword who turned an idea into reality. Jim Morgan, Grace Kane, Auntie Belle, John Page and Mike Borrow who shared their own Blitz memories with me. My team of faithful walkers who tested the routes, drank in the pubs and shared my enthusiasm consisting of Danny and Russell Conboy, John Mogie, Liz Budge, Sarah Abdy, Julian Whippy, Pete Smith and my wife Ali.

Staff at the following resource centres proved most helpful in the loan of photographs and documents, the Metropolitan Police Archives in Charlton, the Bank of England Museum, the National Archives at Kew and Westminster Central Methodist Hall. In addition the following loaned their own personal photographs for use in this book: Ronny Biggs, Alison Harris, John Woolsgrove from the Shellhole in Ypres, Paul Fishwick, Keith Blake and Dave Warren. Finally to Derek Hales, Clive Mendonca and Alan Curbishley for providing twenty years of memories in London, long may they continue.

WALK ONE Bank to London Bridge

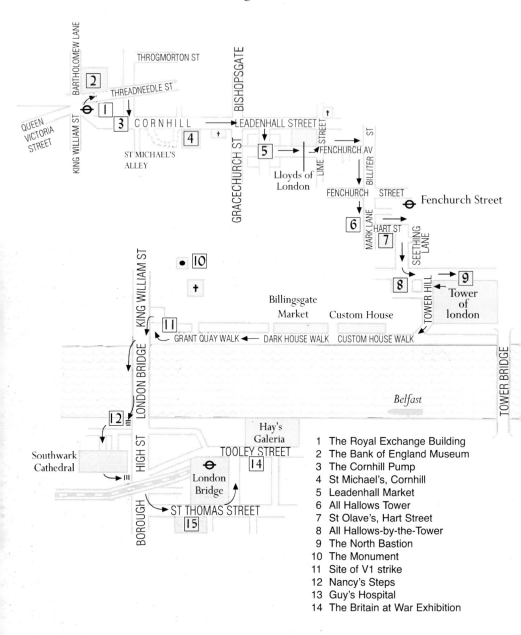

1   The Royal Exchange Building
2   The Bank of England Museum
3   The Cornhill Pump
4   St Michael's, Cornhill
5   Leadenhall Market
6   All Hallows Tower
7   St Olave's, Hart Street
8   All Hallows-by-the-Tower
9   The North Bastion
10 The Monument
11 Site of V1 strike
12 Nancy's Steps
13 Guy's Hospital
14 The Britain at War Exhibition

WALK ONE

Bank to London Bridge

*Starting point – **Bank Station** (Central/Northern/District/Circle Lines)*
*Finish point – **London Bridge Station** (Terminus/Northern Line)*

On arrival at Bank underground station make your way to the booking hall and climb to street level via EXIT 3. The impressive building in front of you is the Royal Exchange, founded by Sir Thomas Gresham to compete with major European market places in 1566. The present building has stood here since 1842 and by 1939 had been converted to office space. It was largely undamaged during the war. A

'The biggest crater in London.' And the same view today

prominent feature during this time was the huge banner proclaiming 'DIG FOR VICTORY'. To begin with turn around and face west. The busy road junction in front of you is one of the main arteries of the city. Part of a seven-way interchange, it includes the crossroads of Threadneedle Street, Cornhill, Poultry and King William Street. Beneath it is the rotunda that makes up the booking hall of Bank tube station. This was once known as 'the biggest crater in London'.

On 11 January 1941 a mixed force of He-111s and Ju-88s, comprising some 145 aircraft, raided the city and dropped over 140 tonnes of high explosive and 21,000 incendiary bombs. At 7.59pm this junction took a direct hit. The bomb tore through the thin street layer and caused the booking hall to collapse. The blast was then driven down the escalator shaft on to the two central line platforms where a large number of people were queuing to use the toilet facilities situated on the upper concourse. In this single incident one hundred and eleven people lost their lives, one of the highest death tolls during the Blitz. Among the members of the civil defence who perished here were PC Arthur Beagley from Greenwich, on duty with the City of London Police, and forty-nine-year-old Kate Barritt, an East Ender from Bethnal Green who worked in the WVS canteen. One shelterer, Dr Leitner, despite being wounded, worked tirelessly administering what basic medical care he could to the injured until the official relief parties reached them an hour later. Neither his actions nor the disaster itself are commemorated here, but are more than worthy of a mention.

Before we leave this spot there is a very impressive monument to the men of the City of London who died in the Great War. Taking care of the traffic, cross over to Threadneedle Street and the Bank of England building to the left of the Royal Exchange. The Bank of England was founded in 1694 but the building standing today was completed between 1936 and 1939. When only just over a year old, it was hit on the night of 9 September 1940 near its south-west corner, damaging the bank's busy telephone exchange and switchboard. Alongside the still bustling entrance is a rather quaint night porter bell that predates the Blitz period and is still in use today. Alas, its speaker tube is no longer functional, according to staff at the museum.

Continuing east along the building turn left into Bartholomew Lane, where you will find the Bank of England Museum. Open weekdays only, between 10am and 5pm, this free museum provides a fascinating review of the history of money and, in the Rotunda room, contains a small but informative display of the Bank in wartime. On show are a number of artefacts, including fragments of incendiaries dropped on the Bank and a collection of good contemporary photographs showing the devastation caused outside by the 11 January incident. Security at the museum is reassuringly tight, but I found the staff most helpful and knowledgeable.

On leaving the museum turn left and at the bottom of Bartholomew Lane to the right is Throgmorton Street. This ancient alley runs behind the Stock Exchange and was the scene of much activity on 16 October 1940. During what was described officially as a 'light raid', a nearby office building caught fire and auxiliary fire fighter Daniel McEvoy and Henry Maclean, a volunteer firewatcher for the premises, were killed during the blaze. That night thirteen German aircraft were destroyed and forty-six Londoners lost their lives.

Returning to Threadneedle Street, use the crossing that takes you to Royal Exchange Buildings, a cut through to Cornhill. A number of the original structures that stood here were destroyed

Throgmorton Street.

The Cornhill Pump.

in the Great Fire of 1666 and this marks the limit of its advance. The Great Fire was a key point in London's long history, a legacy of this being the wide streets we find in the capital today, providing natural firebreaks. This planning policy proved vital during the autumn and spring of 1940/1941. Pass the granite memorial to Paul Reuter whose world news organization was founded near this spot in 1851 and still exists today. On entering Cornhill you see an unusual blue metal structure. This is a water pump on the site of an ancient well and was provided for public use in 1799, following contributions from the Bank of England, the East India Company and local Fire Offices. Whoever paid for it, the

St Michael's Alley.

men of the Auxiliary Fire Service were thankful, as the pump then came into its own, so desperate was the need for water in this area during the Blitz.

Head east down Cornhill and you see a lantern for Old Simpson's Tavern. Standing under this you find a narrow alleyway, Ball Court. Follow this, for the narrow cobbles stretch to a collection of bars and restaurants that provide a rare glimpse of old London that has survived both the great fires of 1666 and 1940. Try to imagine the chaos that would have been caused by one H.E. bomb or a single canister of fire spurting incendiary devices landing here. Fortune has indeed smiled on this place. Continue following the passage through St Michael's Alley until it brings you back out on to Cornhill, passing The Jamaica Inn, site of London's first coffee house, a fashion that swept the capital in the 1700s. The fading notice in the window provides a history of the building and may in fact predate the Blitz as there is no mention of the war.

St Michael's Church is today a peaceful refuge for city workers and an active place of worship. As with all the churches mentioned on the walks in this book, please bear this in mind when visiting. Before entering, note the old pre-war marking for a double water hydrant on the pavement outside the church entrance, a prayer answered for many a fire-fighter sixty years or so ago. On entering the church we find a number of interesting memorials. On the back left wall is a plaque to Mullens & Co, a firm of stockbrokers that remembers its staff who were killed during the war. Near to this can be found the memorial for The County of London Electrical Supply Company, commemorating both wars. This plaque unusually lists more 1939/45 names than those of the Great War. This is perhaps due to the expansion of electricity and increased staff levels between the two wars. London Electricity still has strong links with St Michael's. In addition to holding an annual memorial service, they also provide fresh flowers to be placed here monthly.

Before leaving, notice hanging from the back right wall the colours of the 10th Royal Fusiliers. Recruited from men of the Stock Exchange and a good example of the fact that London also provided 'Pals' battalions, this unit saw action as part of the 37th Division on the Somme, at Arras and Ypres. The roll of honour is contained in a bronze-hinged frame that opens up and provides a poignant reminder of the horrific casualties sustained by a single infantry battalion between 1914-1918.

On leaving the church turn right on Cornhill and continue straight over Bishopsgate into Leadenhall Street. Constantine FitzGibbon described this area in 1940:

> '*The city was a strangely broken horizon of roofs and chimney pots, with blank, bright windows. The Baltic Exchange was magical, the huge empty offices of the insurance companies in Leadenhall Street romantic and pitiful too, for insurance was something that belonged to another age.*' (i)

After a short distance on the right you will see the covered entrance to the old Leadenhall Market; go in. The Romans built their forum on this site and a market has existed here since the 14th century. It takes its name, Leadenhall, from the huge glass and lead roof that adorned it. This was partially damaged during the Great Fire. Its current cover was rebuilt in 1881 by Sir Horace Jones, architect of both Smithfield and Bishopsgate. Despite being a fragile structure, it remained one of the few buildings in this area undamaged during the war, most of its neighbours being totally destroyed. Leave via Leadenhall Lane, left at the Lamb Pub, towards Lime Street. On exiting, look back. The glass façade that marks the eastern entrance to the market was damaged during the Blitz, although this was from a falling anti-aircraft 'rocket shell', not enemy action. It is often suggested by veterans of the civil defence services that the majority of minor injuries caused to them were from falling anti-aircraft shrapnel during the raids.

You are now entering an area of complete devastation from the night of 10/11 May 1941. This night marked the largest and final major raid on the city. The weather was perfect for bombing, with minimal cloud. Over 500 aircraft raided the capital, some crews returning twice to drop their payload of 711 tons of H.E. and over 86,000 incendiaries between 2300 and 0530hrs. A firewatcher on top of the Lloyds building described the scene thus:

The entrance to Leadenhall Market.

'The sky was full of planes in constant procession like bank holiday traffic on the Southend Road.'

As you enter Lime Street all but one of the buildings on the eastern side of the road was gutted. The survivor dates back to 1929 and today, somewhat ironically, houses a German Bank.

On your left the imposing Lloyd's Building is a 'masterpiece' from a different era and is constructed on the spot of the previous Lloyd's premises, Royal Mail House. This huge building, completed in the late 1920s, stood on 1.5 acres of land right in the heart of the city and formed the HQ for zone C3 fireguard during the war. The basements of the building were soon transformed into dormitories and, except during raids, sleeping in offices overnight by staff was permitted. This ensured that the important day-to-day work of Lloyd's of London went ahead. The numbers of shelterers steadily increased as the bombing continued and a growing number of staff found themselves homeless. In addition, a Friends Ambulance Unit Shelter was added, the nightly population in the building reaching over 300.

The company insisted that at least two firewatchers were posted on the roof during a raid and a number of men acting as quick-reaction forces

Lime Street after a raid. and Lime Street sixty years later.

Fenchurch Avenue, 1941.

were on standby within the building. This policy meant that many a night was passed playing rooftop quoits while the watchers had 'nothing to report'. During major raids, however, the men of Lloyd's not only witnessed the destruction of many important buildings such as the Guildhall and the Port of London Authority but also saw the near misses on London Bridge and St Paul's. The fact that the Lloyds building survived the war with only 'shattered windows, doors and honourable scars' is a tribute to the men and women engaged in its civil defence. In the months following 10/11 May Lloyd's stood alone like a giant headstone on the grave of the city.

The records which the staff at Lloyd's kept provide us with an accurate description of the blitz. The following entry is taken from the logbook for the night of 9 October 1940, during which the High Altar of St Paul's was damaged and the city sustained over 400 civilian casualties:

5.56 AM – Stick of four H.E. bombs being dropped overhead, 1st near Mappin & Webb, 2nd in the middle of Cornhill, 3rd in Leadenhall Street, the damage of 1st as yet unknown but 2nd and 3rd fractured gas mains. The 4th demolished Ellerman & Bucknall office. Only damage to Lloyd's building was a few broken windows.

6.30 AM – Three large fires in Shoreditch direction that were under control in a remarkably short space of time.

7.06 AM – All Clear. (ii)

The devastated area around Fenchurch Avenue.

All Hallows Tower.

We leave Lime Street via Fenchurch Avenue turning right into Billiter Street and head south crossing over Fenchurch Street and bear to the right into Mark Lane. The area you have passed through has no building of interest to stop and look at, simply because nothing survived, the entire area being 'coventrated', to use a Luftwaffe contemporary phrase. As you continue south along Mark Lane you reach a solitary Church Tower of obvious age. This stands alone among its modern neighbours as a further reminder of the devastation caused in May 1941. The Tower of All Hallows, Staining, dates back to 1320. It survived the Great Fire, although the adjacent Clothworkers Hall was razed to the ground. The number of burials in the churchyard apparently contributed to the weakening of its foundations and led to the church collapsing in 1671. The church merged with St Olave's in Hart Street in 1870 but the tower is still

The bomb-damaged tower of St Olave's.

maintained by the Clothworkers Company, which first forged links with it over 300 years ago.

Continue down Mark Lane to the junction with Hart Street. Pass the entrance to St Olave's (the patron saint of Norway), right into Seething Lane and, heading south, enter the small courtyard at the rear of the church where a bench can be found. St Olave's appears a number of times in the history of London. Founded in the 11th century this is the fourth building on the spot. It crops up frequently in Samuel Pepys' diary and he is buried in the crypt alongside a number of plague victims and the original Mother Goose. Charles Dickens referred to it as his 'favourite church in London'. The third building on this site was destroyed between April and May 1941. The original fire-damaged brickwork is visible, combined with a more modern structure of 1954. The remains of the tower itself were incorporated in the current building. On leaving St Olave's continue south past the large Naval Office and small fenced-off park where Pepys worked. A number of buildings and alleyways still bear his name. You will then come out onto Byward Street.

Look right; on the night of 10/11 May an out-of-control fire was creeping in your direction from the Great Tower Street and Mark Lane junction and was by now a considerable threat to the Tower itself. The job of saving it fell to an 'old sweat' fire-fighter, Station Officer James Ellis. Unfortunately the promised pumps from Kent had yet to arrive and, with the water mains gone, he desperately needed a hose-laying lorry to relay water from the Thames 200 yards away. Heading west, he went in search of one, but, on locating it, found the driver less than keen to move, saying that the road was impassable. Ellis jumped on the running board and guided the driver:

'Through potholes, over piles of brick, with the flames fanning across the street, where we were almost blinded by drifting dust and the shimmering red reflection. Smeared with soot, my eyes streaming and choking with acrid smoke I arrived at the control point. A somewhat surprised Superintendent Joe Ayling, my chief, asked curiously "Where did you go for that?" "To hell and back" was my reply.' (iii)

Before we leave this area, one last look up Great Tower Street fails to reveal one of the individual tragedies that took place here on the night of 29 December 1940. While most of the city burned under the worst incendiary raid on London of the war, sixteen-year-old Godfrey Emmerson, a boy scout who had enlisted in the Home Guard, died at his home, No 55 Great Tower Street.

Opposite you is All Hallows by the Tower. To reach it take the subway under busy Byward Street. The steps you go down are the entrances to the

original Tower Hill underground station. All Hallows boasts a history comparable with the Tower of London itself, a number of its beheaded victims being laid to rest there. For those with the time a very informative audio tour is available for a small charge. Remember, though, that this is an active place of worship. Tours are only available daily between 10.00 and 16.00hrs and it is closed on Bank Holidays. There has been a church here for over 1300 years and it is the final resting place of many Bishops and Archbishops. This was the spot where Samuel Pepys stood and watched the Great Fire in 1666, but the building was itself to succumb to another Great Fire in 1941 before being rebuilt in 1958. The Vicar during the war years was Tubby Clayton, who was instrumental in setting up the 'Toc-H' Everyman's Club in Poperinghe. He was much loved by

All Hallows by the Tower after a raid in 1940.
All Hallows: cleaning up the debris in front of the altar.

veterans of the Great War and is buried here. Much has been written about him but he can best be summed up by the fact that after the war he kept on his batman, employing him as the family cook and, despite mixing in London's high society, would insist on eating 'trench food' as served by his faithful servant. Anyone with an interest in the Great War should take this opportunity to pay him a visit.

Leaving the church, turn right and follow Byward Street heading towards the Tower. The grand building on the opposite side of the road is the Port of London Authority Building. It took a direct hit during the raid of 10/11 May. In front stands the memorial to merchant seaman missing in both wars. The Tower of London itself takes a full day to go round. For us, though, enter the black iron gates at the top of Tower Hill which give a view of its northern wall. About a third of the way along there is a viewing area. Stop here. Before the war, on the North Bastion was a semi-circular structure similar to those at each corner. This was destroyed by a direct hit on the night of 5 October 1940. Yeoman Warder Sam Reeves was killed in the incident. When the remains of the structure were pulled down much older brickwork was uncovered and the curtain wall was rebuilt on this original line, replacing the Victorian bastion. The more recent brickwork is visible. 5 October marked an improvement in weather for the Luftwaffe crews and enabled them to raid London heavily between 23.00hrs and 06.00hrs. Sam Reeves was one of 45 Londoners killed and 329 injured during that day's raids.

The Port of London Authority Building took a direct hit.

Modern brickwork now replaces the bomb-damaged North Bastion of the Tower of London.

Returning to Tower Hill, head down to the river, passing a row of old red telephone kiosks on your left. Before entering Three Quays Walk notice the small circular structure belonging to the London Hydraulic Company. This was part of an old hydraulic lift, long since in

The Blitz-damaged London Hydraulic Company structure on Tower Hill..

disrepair. Of interest are the shrapnel scars from the blitz that adorn the brickwork, and its twisted lettering; also the War Department stamp on the base. Constantine FitzGibbon witnessed a fire here in 1940:

'I remember one on Tower Hill which was an enormous fire. There were more than eighty pumps working in it altogether, and the pump I was on that night was coupled up doing series pumping with a whole group of pumps, which means that the only man who's needed is the man who works the motor. So the pumps' crews were roaming about Tower Hill in small isolated knots, lying down in shelters and smoking and trying to find a pub which might still be open, or where the landlord, even if it was shut, would give one a drink. The whole effect was curiously disorderly. It reminded me rather of Stendhal's description of the Battle of Waterloo. You didn't know quite what was going on, even though it was your fire.' (iv)

Following Three Quays Walk down to the river, look back and try to imagine the chaotic scene of 10/11 May with the dozens of hoses and pumps trying to force water up to Byward Street, against the continual drone of German aircraft overhead, explosions, falling masonry,

Tower Bridge from Three Quays Walk.

smoke and the flickering red reflections that danced off of every building. At the end of this short stretch you see Tower Pier. This was the scene of a desperate struggle on 11 May 1941. It provided a floating platform for a number of pumps drawing water from the river and providing water as far as Whitechapel. At 2am a bomb fell directly on the pier, sending the fire pumps

spinning into the air before eventually dumping them at the bottom of the Thames. Two firemen were killed. The 100-ton hulk HMS *Tower*, a Naval Patrol Depot moored alongside, was sinking fast. Amazingly, replacement pumps were found and the water supply was only temporarily lost.

Now look out to the river. Here we have spectacular views of Tower Bridge, the south bank and HMS *Belfast*. This cruiser, armed with six-inch guns, saw much action in the last war, notably the sinking of the *Scharnhorst* and at the Normandy landings. Post-war she served in the Far East, finally being decommissioned in the 1960s. Today she acts as a floating maritime museum as part of the Imperial War Museum.

We now follow the Thames path west to London Bridge. The building behind, of 1950s vintage, replaces one which was hit by a heavy 'oil drum' bomb in May 1941 that totally destroyed it. Shortly, we arrive at Custom House. This impressive building was damaged when an H.E. shell landed on its north-east corner in 1941. Just behind it a V1 'doodlebug' struck Lower Thames Street in 1944.

After a short distance you enter Old Billingsgate Walk and across the river is Hay's Wharf, 'the larder of London'. It was so named because it was estimated that 80% of the city's perishable foods passed through here 150 years ago. The huge glass-covered arch enabled the largest tea-clippers to sail in to discharge their cargo on their return from the East Indies and China. One can imagine them gracefully sailing up the Thames before nudging carefully into the arched entrance and unloading their precious cargo to the waiting tea and coffee warehouses that lined the South Bank. By 1939 this was a dry-dock housing Shackleton's experimental vessel *Quest*. Today it is a pleasant shopping and restaurant galleria providing a nice spot to eat on completion of this walk.

Behind you is the old Billingsgate fish market, currently empty. A fine description of the market in wartime is recorded by Negley Farson:

> *'The market opens at 6.30 every morning when the big electric arc-lights go on with a clunk, and the iced fish glisten in their trays. One of the fish porters, "Old Ron", a veteran of 45 years in the industry, kickstarts his day*

Custom House and Billingsgate Market.

with a mixture of rum and milk, claims he often carries a load of 16 stone of fish at a time on his traditional guttered leather hat and complains that the price of fish is more of a concern than the falling German bombs. His colleague, a part-time AFS man who has just come off duty after fighting fires in the docks for 48 hours, backs this theory up and adds, "Never closed my eyes I didn't, but we got it under. Two nights a week I'm off and then I sleep". Their customer, who runs a fish and chip shop, states, "I keeps on frying. I haven't closed my shop during an air raid yet – shrapnel dodgers that's what we are". Cod is long off the menu as an expensive luxury, replaced by a mixture of "Dog-fish", "Rock Salmon"(which isn't a salmon) and "Chow Whitings". All three have to make their daily journey to work across London before the sound of the "All Clear". (V)
Continue following the Thames to Dark House Walk, enter an area of city gardens and then stop. On this spot a V1 flying bomb struck and destroyed the offices that stood here. The event was witnessed by firewatchers

'Old Ron' Billingsgate Fishporter, 1940.

on Lloyds Bank roof. They saw the doodlebug flying up the Thames over Tower Bridge, with a trail of flames spitting from its rear. Then the engine cut out and a few seconds' silence followed, before the whistle of its steep descent. A huge explosion and high column of smoke arose from the vicinity of London Bridge. For a short time they thought the bridge, a major crossing and artery of the City, had gone. It was indeed a close miss. In fact the damage caused by V1s was comparable to that of naval parachute mines used by the Luftwaffe since September 1940. The dramatic fear factor described above, however, made the V1 the terror weapon it was. In total, over 2,400 reached London between June 1944 and March 1945.

Continuing towards the Bridge, the area on your right opens up and gives views of two of London's old landmarks. The church of St Magnus the Martyr was once on the roadway that approached the old London Bridge, sold to an American who apparently bought the wrong one. Behind it is the Golden Monument that commemorates the Great Fire of 1666, which started in nearby Pudding Lane. Both survived the second

Great Fire of London 29 December 1940.

On reaching the present London Bridge take the first stairway on your right. This soon brings you up to street level and the bridge itself outside Adelaide House. Look north towards King William Street and the Monument. The photo below is a similar view taken the morning after a raid in September 1940. At the top of the road on the right stands the entrance to Monument Underground station. These stairs were once surrounded by a hastily constructed blast wall long since gone, which provided basic protection from flying shrapnel and blasting debris from entering the shelters themselves.

Walking over the Thames, our next destination is Southwark Cathedral. On reaching the south bank cross over to the west side of the road. A flight of stairs in front of you goes down below bridge level. These are the only remaining part of the old London Bridge. They also mark the scene of the vicious murder of Nancy by Bill Sykes

King William Street 2002.

King William Street 1940.

in Charles Dickens' *Oliver Twist*.

At the foot of the stairs turn right. The entrance to Southwark Cathedral is just beyond the Mudlark pub via the new Millennium Courtyard. Southwark was only granted cathedral status in 1905 on the formation of a new Anglican Diocese, but the building in part dates back to the 13th Century. Among its famous patrons were William Shakespeare, who lived in this parish for a time, and John Harvard, who was baptised here in 1607 and later went on to found the famous American University. Both are commemorated inside. The Harvard Chapel is an area of quiet reflection and silence should be observed. The chapel has an ornate stained glass window that was blown in during the Blitz and the Harvard family paid for its restoration in 1948. The South Transept contains the laid-up colours of the 3rd and 4th Battalion of the Queen's Royal West Surrey Regiment. On the back wall can also be found a simple stone plaque commemorating the men and women from No 37 (London) Force, National Fire Service, who gave their lives in the service of their country during the Second World War. Close to 400 fire-fighters from both the NFS and AFS were killed in the London region during this period.

Though there is no entrance charge, a donation is appreciated and audio tours and guided tours are available. An interactive exhibition, 'The long view of London', which enables you to view the city's skyline by remote-control cameras, and a film show on the building's history are recent additions, as well as a café, so allow an hour or so for a good look round.

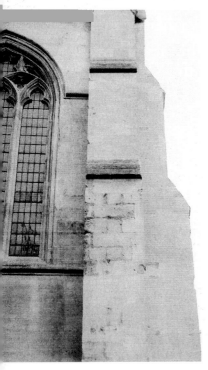

On leaving the Cathedral via its southern exit you emerge into a peaceful churchyard. Note the shrapnel damage on the outside of the Southern Transept. While there were no direct hits on the Cathedral, it did suffer a fair amount of blast damage. It is, after all, squeezed between important railway and river crossings. Climb the steps ahead of you and you are now on Borough High Street. Cross over the road and head right under the railway bridge. After a short while turn left into St Thomas Street and on the right-hand side of the road you will see Guy's Hospital. Thomas Guy, a London bookseller in the early 18th Century, made his fortune from stocks and

Blitz scars on Southwark Cathedral.

1945

Hanslip Fletcher's drawing of the Blitz-damaged Guy's Hospital.

shares prior to the bursting of the South Sea Bubble in 1720. The following year, at the cost of £240,000, he built and endowed this famous hospital. On the evening of 29 December 1940 it suffered a number of fires in an incendiary attack. The nurses' quarters roof was ablaze in three places. These and further outbreaks of fire were dealt with by all available staff members, patients aware of the approaching danger by the flickering flames and surging temperatures on the wards. The brigade were quick to arrive, but hampered by an initial lack of water from nearby hydrants, and it was only after a long and exhausting struggle that a relay link from the river could be established and, despite frequent stoppages, water was available to assist the stricken hospital. Later on in the war the East Wing was totally destroyed. In the 1950s, however, this was rebuilt and the remainder of the original building still stands.

Continuing towards London Bridge Station note the modern design on this part of the terminus. The original was hit on a number of occasions during the war, but two incidents in particular occurred here. On 19-20 April 1941 the first 1,000-tonne raid was launched on London to honour Hitler's birthday and the St Thomas facade was struck by a heavy HE

Bomb damage at London Bridge Station, 1941.

bomb in the early hours of the 20th. Visibility for Luftwaffe crews that evening was hindered by a layer of cloud, meaning that only occasionally were the target areas south of Tower Bridge to the Becton Gasworks in sight. Parachute flares were dropped to aid target location and by 0300hrs large fires were visible in the dock areas and at Greenwich. The damage at London Bridge, however, was caused by one of the bombs which missed its intended target, but its eventual strike was temporarily to take out one of London's major rail terminuses.

Further down St Thomas Street stop at the entrance to Stainer Street, a vaulted road running underneath London Bridge Station. On 17-18

February 1941 a medium-sized raid took place. Forty-three aircraft bombed London, delivering a payload of 42 tons H.E. and 4,600 incendiary bombs. The most serious incident that evening took place in front of you at the entrance to Stainer Street. Many people preferred to take refuge in warehouse basements, church crypts and even in Epping Forest rather than in the public shelters provided during the early stages of the Blitz. The use of underground stations was limited at this time and permanent medical facilities, catering, sanitation and bedding were only just appearing in the recognized tube shelters.

This archway was considered by many to be a safe haven during the bombings and had been used in a similar fashion in the Zeppelin raids of the Great War. The authorities, though acknowledging this, attempted to discourage its use in favour of purpose-built shelters. At 2250hrs on the 17th a direct hit near to the St Thomas Street entrance tore through the surface layer, blocking the archway and entombing the occupants for several hours in tons of fallen masonry and brickwork. Rescue work continued for hours and, when finally cleared, revealed ninety fatalities. An added tragedy was the unnoticed delayed-action bomb lying nearby

The aftermath of the Stainer Street incident, February, 1941.

The 'Britain at War' Exhibition.

that went off during the rescue operation and killed two workers several hours after the initial incident.

Walk through Stainer Street (though this is not recommended after dark). Today it is a busy roadway that contains a number of bonded warehouses and lockups. The strip lighting, damp peeling walls and darkened entrances all add to the eerie atmosphere of this place. When trying to imagine the disastrous events of 62 years ago, nowhere on this walk is it easier to feel the Blitz. It is all around you and an overwhelming sadness prevails. On coming out onto Tooley Street and rejoining modern-day London it seems appropriate to end our journey.

Somewhat surreally you are greeted with a sign proclaiming 'This Way to the Air Raid Shelter'. This takes you to the privately run 'Britain at War Exhibition', open between 10.00hrs and 16.30hrs daily. There is a charge, but it proves to be a fascinating museum dedicated to life in the Blitz, complete with a dummy V2 rocket attached to the wall.

Now you are just a short way from the queuing tourists waiting to enter the London Dungeons before you reach the entrance to the Underground Station at London Bridge.

(i) *The Blitz* – Constantine FitzGibbon – Ditchling Press 1957

(ii) *Lloyds Under Fire* – Lloyds 1947

(iii) *The City That Wouldn't Die* – Richard Collier – Collins 1959

(iv) *The Blitz* – Constantine FitzGibbon – Ditchling Press 1957

(v) *Bombers Moon* – Negley Farson – Victor Gollancz Ltd 1941

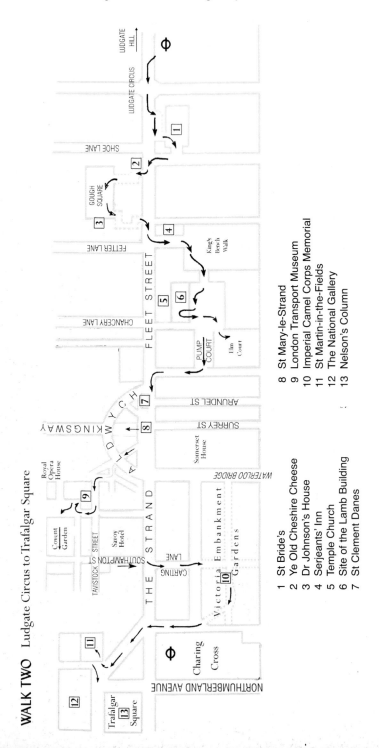

WALK TWO Ludgate Circus to Trafalgar Square

1 St Bride's
2 Ye Old Cheshire Cheese
3 Dr Johnson's House
4 Serjeants' Inn
5 Temple Church
6 Site of the Lamb Building
7 St Clement Danes
8 St Mary-le-Strand
9 London Transport Museum
10 Imperial Camel Corps Memorial
11 St Martin-in-the-Fields
12 The National Gallery
13 Nelson's Column

WALK TWO

Ludgate Circus to Trafalgar Square

*Starting Point – **City Thameslink** (Thameslink Service)*
*Finish Point – **Charing Cross Underground** (Northern/Bakerloo Lines)*

On leaving the station turn left on to Ludgate Hill and head west down the hill and away from St Paul's Cathedral. This is covered in full in another walk. The first junction you arrive at is Ludgate Circus. For centuries this has been a hive of activity and is immortalized in numerous paintings and picture postcards. Today the railway bridge has gone, as the present line runs under the road junction. The bridge actually survived the

Ludgate Circus in 1914 and today.

war but a number of the buildings, including what is now the station, were reduced to rubble. Douglas Reed described the scene in December 1940,

'It was a fantastic sight. Numbers of people were in the streets. Ludgate Hill, with the railway bridge running across it, shone as bright as day in the glare and the dome of St Paul's stood out gigantic against the red sky, with flames licking at it from all sides. Here as an office boy and clerk and journalist I had spent many of my days and nights, before and after the Great War, but I had never thought to see a second fire of London there'. (i)

Staying on the south of the road you cross New Bridge Street (a left turn here would take you to Blackfriars Bridge) and you are now in Fleet Street. Look back at Ludgate Circus once more. Journalist Charles Graves describes the aftermath of a raid here:

'We walked up Ludgate Hill, stepping over hoses, with the dank smoky smell unmistakably coming from burnt-out buildings that had been well and truly spurted by the Fire Brigade. Numbers of city workers walked about with dazed and stunned looks. They were the people who had arrived the previous morning and found that their place of employment was gutted and were coming back the following day to stare at the ruins simply because they had nothing better to do and because it was such a habit to go to the office from their suburbs. Firemen were still hard at work, smoke and steam rose in various directions and each of those charming little alleyways, once the haunt of publishers, was full of policemen and firemen in high boots.' (ii)

The Steeple of St Bride's.

Our first stop, St Bride's, is reached via the narrow Bride's Lane, its spire being visible from the main road. This church, considered as one of Wren's finest, replaced its predecessor, which was destroyed in the great fire of 1666. It is famous for its tiered spire. A local pastry chef, William Rich, who lived at No 3, Ludgate Hill, overlooked the church and was inspired by the unique steeple to design his fashionable wedding cakes, a tradition that still exists today.

The church was gutted during the incendiary attack of 29 December 1940 and was not completely rebuilt until 1957. It had made the fatal error of not manning a fire squad; struck by incendiaries early in the raid, staff at the nearby Press Association and Reuter's News Service entered the blazing church to recover whatever they could; several trips enabled them to save a number of precious items including a brass lectern that had survived the 1666 fire. As they left for the last time the roof of St Bride's came down behind them in a pile of smouldering masonry.

Inside, a number of items commemorate the building's wartime experiences, including a tablet to Rector Cyril Moxon Armitage, a man whose faith and hard work led to the rebuilding. Another, this time on one of the wooden panels that line the south wall, records with classical British understatement:

'Those anxious days of 1940 – 1941 when both the City Temple and St Bride's were devastated by enemy air action, both groups of worshippers met here under the guidance of Rev Weatherhead and Rev Taylor.'

The large and impressive mural painting above the high altar was taken from the design of Christopher Wren himself. This was his visual interpretation of Hutton's 'New view of London', which first appeared in 1706, the current mural having been given by the city firm of Garden & Gotch in their centenary year of 1953.

As previously mentioned, by 1945 only the outer walls and steeple stood, and one of the interesting areas uncovered by the bombings was found in the crypt. Now a free (donations accepted) museum, it reveals the different periods of London life via the rock and debris strata right down to Roman street level. This fascinating little exhibition contains a number of Blitz-related pieces, including German shell fragments, newspapers and an incredible photograph showing the area you have so far walked. Before leaving St Bride's a visit to the side altar, where candles are permanently lit, serves to show the often forgotten side to modern journalism, the danger that some reporters put themselves in to bring us news of modern-day conflicts. The close proximity of Fleet Street has led to St Bride's being the adopted church of the newspaper and media world.

We leave via the glass doors and right into Salisbury Court. This leads back out on to Fleet Street, a vivid description of which in December 1940 is provided by Ritchie Calder:

'The rooftops of Fleet Street seemed a stockade of flames. The Middle Temple Library was hopelessly alight, Johnson's London, those narrow backcourts that are the hinterland of Fleet Street, was a flaming acre. Part of the Daily Telegraph *building was burning furiously. The Spire of St Bride's, parish church of journalism, was a macabre Christmas tree festooned in fire, and its inner pillars burning like candles.'* (iii)

Thankfully, some of the surrounding buildings did survive and today opposite you is found a wonderfully eclectic mix of architecture from the marvellous art-deco building complete with colourful clock that was occupied by the *Daily Telegraph*, alongside which is the Victorian façade of the King & Keys, then a Tudor building that now houses a modern-day sandwich bar, and finally one of the remaining famous ancient London pubs, Ye Olde Cheshire Cheese. Throughout the winter nights of 1940 this street was congested, not with a mix of businessmen and tourists, but Fire and Civil Defence workers trying to prevent the spread of flames from fanning their way up this wide thoroughfare and destroying more of the buildings that surround you. Between September and December 1940 London was subjected to almost ninety days of continual raids.

Fleet Street architecture.

The marvel of Fleet Street during the war was that, despite the bombings, the press continued to function. Hardly an edition of a London newspaper was missed. Deep beneath every office could be found emergency pressrooms, editorial offices and composing rooms. Telegraph wires were buried to enable the news to get through regardless of the situation above ground. The rooftops of every building housed spotters in small sandbagged enclosures. One night in

Roof spotters above Fleet Street.

September 1940 the two men on the *Evening Standard* building had a narrow escape when a bomb fell down the lift shaft next to them, damaging a lower floor. Cross Fleet Street and follow Hind Court, a narrow alleyway found to the left of the Ye Olde Cheshire Cheese. A short signposted walk leads us to the house of Dr Samuel Johnson, who is credited not with writing the first English dictionary, but one that became a standard work until the Oxford English appeared at the turn of the 20th century. This small literary landmark was under threat in December 1940 when a fire in a factory building in Gough Square threatened to spread to the surrounding block. In the upper floors of Dr Johnson's house a fire broke out and, armed only with sand, fire-fighters were able to bring the blaze under control, thus saving the two-hundred-year-old building.

Dr Johnson's house.

Return to Fleet Street, head right as far as the junction with Fetter Lane. This ancient street, where Roman artefacts have been uncovered, is still subject to debate over the origin of its name. The word 'fetter' could derive from the name for a chainmail vest manufactured nearby for members of the Knights Templar, or from a derivation of 'feuriers', or felt makers, who also had workshops in the vicinity. Historians have put numerous other explanations forward; perhaps we will never know its true meaning. What is fact, however, is that it was almost entirely destroyed by May 1941 after a number of raids took their toll of the old buildings. On 9 October 1940 a surface shelter in Fetter Lane was hit and there were a number of fatalities; perhaps the saddest were those of Florence, Muriel and Dorothy Turner, a mother and two daughters; all three lived in this street; at this time, despite government reassurances, the population in general had no real trust in surface shelters and this tragedy did nothing to assist local concerns as to their safety.

Now take the archway opposite that leads into Old Mitre Court. To your left is a smart courtyard block known as Serjeants' Inn. The Serjeants, a superior order of barrister who supplied Common Law Judges, once lived

Serjeants' Inn 1941.

here. By the start of the war, however, it belonged to the Incorporated Council of Law Reporting. Struck by a combination of high explosives and incendiaries, the building was reduced to a pile of rubble in May 1941.

You are now entering the area collectively known as the Temple, which contains an Inner and Outer Temple. The complex was originally an outpost for the Knights Templar, an order founded to protect pilgrims journeying to the Holy Lands. After their downfall in the 14th Century the premises were in disrepair and lawyers began to move in. Today it houses two of London's four Inns of Court. The first, Mitre Court Buildings, was destroyed during a raid in May 1941. A plaque on the wall records this. In fact nearly all the buildings that line King's Bench Walk date from the 1950s, testament to the damage sustained here. A number of fatalities occurred in this area that evening, among them a local resident and lawyer John Adrian Porteigle Ament. Aged fifty-six, he was injured and evacuated, later dying of his wounds at St Bartholomew's Hospital.

On the side of No 1 it is stated that in 1949 King George VI opened the building as a temporary library until a more permanent structure could be found. The new library today stands opposite.

The American journalist Basil Woon describes the scene in September 1940;

> *'The first thing I hear when I go out is that the Temple was hit last night, I charter a taxicab to get down there and heave a sigh of relief when I come to Pump Court and find it intact. But the Middle Temple library, probably the finest law library in the world, suffered a direct hit, it is in ruins, its clock tower leaning crazily at an angle. Even though most of the valuable books were sent away at the beginning of the war the loss is serious. The bomb had missed my friend Pritt's chambers by about sixty yards.'* (iv)

Take the archway to the right of the library that leads to an open courtyard. This was the site of the ancient Lamb building, built in 1667 and destroyed on 11 May 1941 when a raid of over 500 aircraft bombed the capital. They dropped over 700 tons of H.E. and 86,000 incendiary devices, mainly in this area, the second massive fire blitz within six months. A tablet set in the ground makes reference to this fact and another modern structure stands behind it. The column you see was put up in 2000 and marks the spot where the Great Fire of 1666 came to a standstill, to complement Wren's monument in Pudding Lane where the fire began. Facing west, in the left-hand corner of this courtyard is a small entrance that takes you down some stairs into a garden, sheltered and complete with water feature. This was Fig Tree Court, destroyed in 1666, rebuilt in 1679 and then destroyed again by enemy air action in 1940. Pause for a while and then return to the main courtyard from where you can enter the circular Temple church.

The ancient Lamb Building, 1667-1941

This is one of the oldest churches in London, dating from 1185. The outside of the building does look old; only the 'pepper pot' roof was replaced after the war.

However, the more modern restored interior is a result of it being almost entirely burnt out during the Blitz. On entering, to your left are a number of stone effigies set in the circular floor. These commemorate some of the original knights who are buried here. They have lain in this format for over 160 years since a restoration in 1841. Around them on the walls

The plaque where the building once stood.

The Temple Church before it lost its 'pepper pot' steeple in May 1940.

are inscribed the names of the men of the Inner Temple who lost their lives in both world wars. There is also a small plaque to Walter Godfrey and his son, the architects who restored and partly rebuilt the church after the war. Similarly, in the main body of the church it is recorded that the Archbishop of Canterbury rededicated it in 1954. When fire tore through the building on the night of 10 May 1941 all the wooden interior, the roof and the organ were completely destroyed, molten lead dripped on to the effigies and surviving pillars. This is recorded both in a stained glass window depicting St Paul's Cathedral at the height of the raid and a painting by the artist Kathleen Allen which can be seen in the porch of the church as you leave.

On leaving the church exit the courtyard by heading through a series of arches to your right and into Pump Court. Compare the view with the wartime photograph. All the buildings on the left-hand side have been rebuilt. As you emerge at the far end into Brick Court head right up towards the 'headroom 11ft' sign which will bring you back out onto

Pump Court, 1941.

The Royal courts of Justice.

Fleet Street almost opposite the Royal Courts of Justice; then turn left towards the Strand. The Royal Courts have stood here since 1882. They and the Old Bailey were both damaged by enemy air action in April 1941. On your left are the premises of Twining's, with an elaborate entrance. The oldest surviving tea dealers in the country, they have had a shop here since 1706. On 12 January 1941 a single bomb landed in Devereux Court to the rear of this spot, destroying Twining's offices and warehouse. A fire caught hold and the building was completely destroyed. A two-hundred-year-old Matthew Dutton clock was salvaged from the rubble and keeps good time to this day.

Our next stop is straight ahead. By crossing to the traffic island you find yourself at the back wall of St Clement Danes. Since the ninth century a church for the local Danish community has stood here. Rebuilt by William the Conqueror, this historic building was totally gutted by incendiary devices on the night of 10 May 1941. The shrapnel damage is still evident on the wall to the right of the church. After the war, when the building lay in ruins, the Royal Air Force paid for its renovation and today it acts as their main church of Remembrance. At the front of the building two bronze statues flank the entrance. Hugh Dowding and Arthur Harris, commanders of Fighter and Bomber Command respectively, face towards the Aldwych. The church closes between 1500 and 1600 hours. When open, allow half an hour to browse among the numerous memorials and

St Clement Danes.

items of interest inside. Every RAF unit has its Squadron badge embossed on the floor tiles; a map at the entrance will help you identify a particular squadron. The roll of honour for all personnel killed in both wars is found in leather-bound books on either side of the main altar. A number of personal items are shown in cabinets and a list of every RFC and RAF Victoria and George Cross winners is also on display.

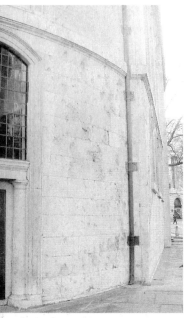

Shrapnel damage to the side wall of St Clement Danes.

As you leave head up the Aldwych to the left of Australia House. This was once the location of an EWS (emergency water supply) that contained 11,000 gallons of water; a great number of these temporary structures could be found in city streets; however, no traces remain today. Underneath us runs a disused underground tunnel. The old station entrance is still visible opposite. This deep tunnel was used to store treasures from the British Museum during the war years. It also provided nightly shelter for several thousand Londoners and was the scene of a number of concerts provided by the Entertainments National Service Association or, as it was more commonly known, ENSA. The track itself was boarded over and rows of bunk beds added. It was the blueprint for a further seventy-nine tube stations by the winter of 1940.

The next building we see is Bush House, home of the BBC World Service. The BBC moved their empire service here in 1941 after a 500lb bomb damaged part of Broadcasting House and has remained here ever since. From this building the

Aldwych emergency water supply.

BBC broadcasted to millions of Europeans living under Nazi occupation. With coded messages for resistance movements and broadcasts to our boys overseas, it became an integral part of the war effort. Expansion during this period led to the BBC broadcasting in over forty-five foreign languages, in addition to the twenty-four-hour service in English. It was during the war that the BBC gained its international reputation for accurate and impartial reporting. It was from here that the exiled General De Gaulle spoke to the French people urging them to 'resist the occupying forces', and it was from here that my good friend Grace Kane, now in her eighties, came to record a goodwill message for her husband John, a Royal Engineer serving overseas. She still recalls the stage fright she felt when 'the on-air light came on and a smart-suited man announced, "This is London calling our boys in Burma with messages from home..."' She also remembers the homely looking middle-aged lady in front of her who, with a broad Norfolk accent, said, 'Come home soon Billy. Your mum's got a nice pudding waiting for you, son'. This building is leased by the

Entrance to the now disused Strand Underground Station.

A view of the Strand just before

BBC from a Japanese company and its future is uncertain when the lease runs out in 2005. For many Londoners it is an iconic reminder of London's past.

The well-stocked bookshop offers much nostalgia, with recordings of wartime shows and a good selection of history books. Bush House was itself damaged by a V1 rocket on 30 June 1944. We will look at this later.

Another small church in front of us as we continue west is St Mary-le-Strand. This church, which today serves as the church of the Women's Royal Naval Service, was one of the few buildings to emerge from the blitz relatively undamaged. This may in part be due to the gallant efforts of Jim Morgan and his colleagues in the AFS. Jim joined his local Auxiliary station underage in 1939, but was offered a position as a messenger boy and used to ride out of the station (a half-built car showroom) on the footplate of the escape pump whenever the bells went down. He would pass his house, his proud mother waving goodbye. As time went on the messenger boys were trained to man relay pumps and ensure the water supply reached the fire-fighters grasping the branches and trying to quench the fire. This was not always an easy task with water in such short supply. When it had to be brought up from the Thames this may have involved four such relay pumps before the water reached the men at the front.

St Mary-le-Strand today.

One evening in May 1941 Jim found himself performing that role on exactly this spot. His pump was parked outside the entrance to the church where today stands a traffic island. Just sixteen years old, alone and in the middle of a raid, he worked tirelessly to keep the pump in action as the fire appeared to creep nearer and nearer him from the direction of St Clement Danes. Every so often the water would stop and a panic would ensue. Only later was he to discover that the fault lay at the water's edge. The suction hoses that had earlier been fitted with copper filters had recently been replaced with cheaper wicker filters; these frequently clogged up with the mud of the Thames and had to be cleaned out by hand. Jim remembers looking up towards the fire, still some distance away, but it felt uncomfortably hot and he could make out branches of hoses from the upper floors of offices pouring water into a wall of fire heading his way. He was unsure if men were on the end of them or if the branches had in fact been lashed to the windows, as was common practise. Any concerns for his own safety were overridden by the sound of falling masonry from the roof of Somerset House, still standing today. The sound of unsynchronized aircraft engines told him that raiders were still overhead and the constant falling of anti-aircraft shrapnel made him sink deeper into his steel helmet. Finally, just as daylight was breaking, the aircraft noises stopped and a relief crew arrived on the scene. Only then was there time for reflection and an opportunity to survey the chaotic war-torn streets around him. London was now definitely in the front line.

A visit to the church reveals a number of interesting war memorials. One of them, the Parish Roll of Honour from the Great War, names Boy Scout Edward Howard who was killed in an enemy air raid on 13 October 1915. This night saw one of the most spectacular Zeppelin and airship raids on the capital. That evening the L.15, commanded by *Kapitanleutnant* Joachim Breithaupt, dropped twenty-eight 110lb explosive and fifteen incendiary bombs over London and the South East, killing twenty-eight people. Part of his route that night took him from Charing Cross up the Strand, the Aldwych and over the Royal Courts of Justice, in essence following our walk in reverse. One of his victims was Scout Edward Howard.

A casualty being treated in the Aldwych, 30 June 1944.

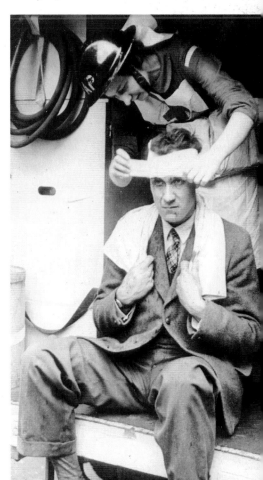

Follow the road west until you reach Montreal Place. Cut through to the Indian High Commission. A plaque here commemorates the spot where DC Jim Morrison (Queen's Gallantry Medal) of the Metropolitan Police died on 13 December 1991, after being fatally stabbed. He was attempting to arrest a thief he had chased from nearby Covent Garden while off duty.

You are now opposite the Waldorf Hotel. Look right. This is the spot where a V1 fell on 30 June 1944. It struck the road surface outside the Air Ministry buildings around midday; forty-eight people were

The aftermath of a V1 Rocket.

killed, mostly passers-by, and a hundred and fifty more were injured, making it one of the most serious flying bomb incidents of the war. When the emergency services arrived they were greeted with a scene of total devastation as the dust settled. Everywhere were strewn the bodies of the dead and wounded. A line of parked London Buses was reduced to a pile of twisted metal and the pavement was littered with money blowing around in the breeze. Though there is a degree of blast damage still visible on some buildings it is difficult to imagine the scene today.

Now cross over, taking care, as the traffic here can get hectic, and enter Exeter Street EC2. We are now entering the heart of London's theatre-land. During the early days of the Blitz when London was bombed nightly people were stuck in the theatres and cinemas while a raid went on outside. Often this led to an impromptu performance by the cast or orchestra until it was considered safe to leave. Soon the continuous raids meant that evening entertainment became impossible and a week after the bombing started only two theatres remained open, with ninety percent of the industry out of work. With matinee performances struggling to attract crowds, most of the profit-making productions went on tour to the provinces. Cinemas still had a role to play. *The Wizard of Oz* packed houses throughout the war, with the audience sighing in unison as the film famously turned from black and white into colour. It somehow acted as an escape from the grey and dusty scene that was London in wartime. One of the larger picture houses would flash an announcement onto the screen at the beginning of each performance:

'WHEN AN AIR-RAID WARNING IS RECEIVED, YOU WILL BE INFORMED FROM THE STAGE. THOSE WISHING TO LEAVE WILL HAVE SEVEN MINUTES TO FIND SHELTER. FOR THOSE DESIRING TO REMAIN THE SHOW WILL GO ON. WALK, NOT RUN TO THE EXITS. DO NOT PANIC. REMEMBER YOU ARE BRITISH!'

Before we cross over into Wellington Street look left at the view over Waterloo Bridge, immortalized in the forties film of the same name starring Vivien Leigh. Like the other bridges that spanned the river, by a combination of hard work and luck it was not hit, but was often the scene of fire pumps, exhausted crews, hose-laying lorries and the debris of war. Nevertheless it remained open.

In Wellington Street at the junction with Tavistock Street can be found an old building that once housed the offices of Charles Dickens. It is now a restaurant. Turn left here into Tavistock Street. You are still following the route taken by the L15 and its crew in 1915 and a number of her bombs were also dropped near here. Our destination is the London Transport Museum and is well signposted. The entrance is found in the main Piazza of Covent Garden. Originally the nineteenth century building was the flower market, but when this moved in the 1970s it was restored and converted to its current role, the museum opening in 1980. The admission price is not cheap at £5.95 for an adult, but concessions are available and children under

The Covent Garden entrance to the London Transport Museum.

sixteen are admitted free when with a paying adult. The opening times are from 10-1800 hrs daily except Fridays when it opens at 1100 and is closed between 24-27 December. This vast collection of vehicles and ephemera includes a wartime bus complete with blast netting and the message:

'I hope you don't mind my interjection, but that stuff there is for your protection' to prevent people peeling it off. A common reply in graffiti went along the lines of 'Thank you for your information but I cannot see my destination!'

In addition to other blitz-related items there is a single-decker bus that was converted to a wartime ambulance, a highlight of the museum being the role-playing staff that come alive and describe their working conditions during various periods of history.

During the war years London Transport played a key role in everyday life and provided far more than just the shelter of the tubes. As early as 1937 an Air Raid Precautions committee had been set up in the company, training staff in fire-fighting, rescue work and first aid. Over 16,000 female employees were taken on during the war and they filled a far wider spectrum of positions than during the Great War, except for driving, which still remained an all-male affair. When hostilities broke out the programme of modernization was halted; the primary role was now to keep London moving even during air raids. Transport services were greatly reduced, thus saving fuel. On the Underground a system of floodgates and watertight doors was installed to reduce the chance of flooding from the Thames due to enemy action.

In 1939 London Transport played a significant part in the mass evacuation of children out of the capital. A number of disused stations were taken over by official bodies such as the London Transport Board and the government-appointed National Railway Executive Committee. Brompton Road station became the operations centre for General Pile's Anti-Aircraft Command. The newly constructed rail depot at Aldenham was converted into a Halifax Bomber factory. Elsewhere workshops constructed parts for armoured vehicles and landing craft and a Home Guard unit was raised, numbering some 30,000 personnel at its height. Quite rightly, though, it is the use of tube stations that remains firmly in the public mind. Despite early concerns in official circles, the public in effect took over a number of shelters and steps were taken to provide efficient sanitation and sleeping, feeding and first-aid facilities below ground.

On leaving the museum come back out into Covent Garden. Today it is an energetic mix of boutiques, bars and street entertainers that gets crowded with tourists and locals, but its history as a market for London dates back to the 1630s when the then Duke of Bedford acquired the land from Westminster Abbey. It was previously the 'Convent Garden'. It became the first public square and an example of town planning when designed by Inigo Jones, who based it on Italian piazzas. By the late nineteenth century it had established itself as London's major fruit, vegetable and flower market, though by the time of the Blitz it was already apparent that a new, larger premises would be required. The market survived almost intact throughout the war with only minor incidents occurring. Basil Woon recalls one such incident in his 1941 reportage of the Blitz 'Hell came to London',

> *' A bomb fell near Covent Garden last night, but I have just threaded my way through the market and have found it piled high with cabbages, tomatoes, oranges, potatoes and other such foods, and life going on as usual. All the bomb did was destroy one small wholesaler's premises and damage the rear of a rather famous old pub. When my barber said to me they got Covent Garden I had visions of shattered stalls, broken market baskets, a giant pot-pourri of mixed vegetables, and chaos everywhere. But not a pane of the glass roof over the Garden is even cracked, and the Opera House stands as of yore.'* (v)

The famous Opera House has recently undergone a major refurbishment. Prior to this the stage sets were famously lifted into place by machinery using a Great War submarine engine. During the last war the Opera House was converted into a dance hall and it was here that the talented saxophonist and clarinet player Ivy Benson formed her all-girl big band in 1939. They went on, against all the odds in a male-dominated environment, to become the BBC resident band. Among the difficulties Ivy had to deal with was material for costumes, parachute silk being utilized on numerous occasions, and also the occupational hazard of her musicians running off and marrying American GIs.

In Covent Garden can be found St Paul's Church outside which Samuel Pepys first witnessed a Punch and Judy show in 1662, suggesting that street theatre has always taken place here. The nearby Lamb & Flag pub was famous for its bare-knuckle fights that took place in the seventeenth century and flower seller Eliza Doolittle of *My Fair Lady* fame worked here.

As we leave the market area via Southampton Street back out into the Strand, in front of us appear two famous wartime eating houses, firstly Simpson's and, next door, the Savoy Hotel and Restaurant, as exclusive today as it was in wartime. Its entrance was damaged in early November 1940 when a number of windows above the famous silver crusader were blown out. An earlier incident here, however, caused even more concern for the authorities. Communist agitators were quick to demonstrate against what they called the 'scandalous lack of public shelters'. They held the view that, while working-class Londoners were being forgotten about in the grand plan, rich folk were being offered safety via the deep and comfortable shelters of London's top hotels and restaurants. It was indeed true that some establishments would advertise their menus and forthcoming attractions alongside the promise of the 'safest shelters in town'.

On 15 September 1940 they organized around a hundred people largely from the East End and marched them to the Savoy with the intention of storming the shelter once the sirens sounded. But any threat of a class war was quickly averted by the all clear, whereupon the participants filed back out onto the street again, but not before a collection had been made to tip the head porter. Bemused by the actions of their working class comrades, the Communist organizers called off their demonstration. It is often forgotten that the Savoy Palace building that once stood on this spot was used as a military prison for deserters awaiting execution in Hyde Park. In 1761 a mutiny involving some two hundred inmates broke out and an innocent bystander was mistaken for a rioter and shot in the ensuing battle.

Take Carting Lane to the right of another old pub, The Coal Hole, and head down towards the river. This narrow street is typical of those used by the fire services to relay much-needed water up from the Thames. Looking at the patches of new tiling on the side of the Savoy Hotel, it would seem to have been a hairy spot when shrapnel and incendiary bombs started to fall. A plaque on the side of the theatre records how it was the first public building in the world to be lit by electricity. Of note when we reach the end of Carting Lane is the crushed drainpipe marked 'Savoy 1881'. On closer examination it looks to have part-melted under intense heat. It may be damage caused by a 'white van man', but remember Hitler passed this way also. It is up to you to decide.

Cross straight over into one of London's most tranquil and forgotten parks, Victoria Embankment Gardens. Divided into various parts, it stretches from Westminster to Temple and is crammed full of statues depicting the great and the good, among them Air Marshal Lord Trenchard, founder of the Royal Air Force in April 1918, General Sir James Outram, hero of the Siege of Lucknow during the Indian Mutiny, General Charles Gordon, who was killed at Khartoum in 1885, and Major General Wingate, Commander of the Chindit force which fought in the Far East in the Second World War. In addition are two memorials which are of more esoteric interest – Samuel Plimsoll, who gave his name to the load line found on shipping and known thereafter as 'the sailor's friend', and a very

Firewatchers on the roofs overlooking the Embankment.

fine memorial dedicated to the men of the Imperial Camel Corps who served in the Middle East during the Great War. We pass to the right of this to leave the park, but, before doing so, when adjacent to an imposing monument and water-lily garden to Major General Cheylesmore, stop and look back. The large clockface behind you belongs to the Shellmex Building. During an air raid on 2 October 1940, the lightest since the Blitz had started, George Gilbert, a sixty-year-old employee acting as a Fire Watcher on the roof, was one of only seven Londoners that night killed by enemy air action. It was from the rooftop of this building that Winston Churchill once took his dinner guests out to watch a raid in progress. From here could be seen a wonderful view of the South Bank and the river:

> '*At least a dozen fires were burning on the south side, and while we were there several heavy bombs fell, one near enough for my friends to pull me back behind a substantial stone pillar. This certainly confirmed my opinion that we should have to accept many restrictions upon the ordinary amenities of life.*' (vi)

When you leave the park the large gate marks the old river's edge before

Charing Cross Station in 1914.

this area was reclaimed in Victorian times when the Embankment was built. A drawing and history of this is displayed as you leave the park and turn right into Villiers Street.

We head up the hill passing the building that was once home to Rudyard Kipling.

On our left is Charing Cross Station and Hotel. In December 1940 a landmine landed on and became entangled in the signals of the track above you. These 1,500-pound high explosive bombs were capable of devastating destruction if set off. Fortunately its parachute and cables had prevented it from hitting the track. However, it was now dangling precariously above a row of burning railway carriages. Firemen hosed the mine down continuously to keep it cool while others fought the fire among the rolling stock below. It was all they could do until Royal Naval explosive experts arrived from Portsmouth early the next morning and by the rush hour the device was safe and this main line terminus was back in use.

Soon the entrance to the Underground Station is reached. On 8 October 1940 London was raided and a number of large fires were started in the city. During that night one shelterer here lost his life, Wilfred Uffindell. The first tube station to be hit is generally thought to be the nearby Trafalgar Square station on 12 October, so perhaps Wilfred died as a result of an accident and not through enemy action.

At the top of the hill you come back out onto the Strand and the impressive frontage of the station. Originally Sir Edward Hungerford, who gives his name to the railway bridge that crosses the Thames behind the station, owned this site. Despite losing most of his fortune by gambling, and his mansion that once stood here destroyed in a fire in 1669, he reputedly lived to the ripe old age of 115. The station itself was built in 1863 with a five- storey luxury hotel on top. At the front is a reproduction of an Eleanor Cross. The original stood where Charles I now sits astride his horse in Trafalgar Square. During the Great War this station was the regular spot for wounded to arrive back in London from the Front. A painting in the Imperial War Museum by J.Hodgson Lobley depicts the impressive façade of the building with a military ambulance ferrying men past a thronging mass of flag-waving people proclaiming a victory on the Somme. Daniel Defoe, who wrote *Robinson Crusoe*, was once put in the stocks on this spot for writing a controversial anti-Protestant pamphlet, but his supporters threw flowers at him instead of rotten fruit.

Cross over into Duncannon Street which will take you up to Trafalgar Square. When you reach the corner of St Martin-in-the-Fields churchyard and the Oscar Wilde bench look back once more at the Station. In the original building two ornate domes sat on top of the roof. These have since been replaced with two forties brick-built structures. They look suspiciously like fire-watching shelters but so far I have been unable to clarify this. Enter the crypt of St Martin's via a flight of stairs. The first chapel on your right has a memorial entrance to the original B.E.F. of 1914. The crypt today is a vibrant café, bookshop and brass-rubbing centre which portrays little of its wartime self. Indeed the stone commemorating its use as a public shelter is partially obscured by the shelving of the gift shop.

St Martin-in-the-Fields has long had a tradition of caring for the poor of London. It first opened its crypt as an air raid shelter to the public in 1916 under the guidance of Dick Sheppard. After the Great War its doors remained open and canteen, medical and welfare facilities were established for up to five hundred homeless people. It seemed natural that during the Blitz people would return to the crypt. On any night up to several hundred people gathered here and tried to sleep as best they

'Shelterers in the crypt of St Martin-in-the-Fields'.

could through the raids. They came from all spectrums of London society and the shelter took on an almost club-type atmosphere over the long nights of 1940-41. Regulars would return to the same spot night after night, where somehow they found a comfort and protection not available in their local surface or tube shelter. The scene is well described by Negley Farson:

'There was a grey-haired old man sitting stiffly on a hard chair, who did not change his posture from ten that night to six the next morning; he had a scholarly distinguished face and there was something about his bearing, his clothes with that air of genteel respectability which made you certain he was a librarian or bookseller. Beside him flat on the stone floor made of ancient tombstones sprawled a navvy, husky, red-faced, sleeping the sleep of an honest working man, blowing intermittent snores of beer. Unmistakable were the Ladies of the Night, members of the oldest profession, as no person was barred from here, and whilst some of the sheltering troops (for passing troops also find it hard to find a bed in London) might have cast longing eyes at them, none of the other women in the crypt turned up their noses, though most of them were middle class.' (vii)

During the war the padre, Pat McCormick, himself awarded a DSO for bravery in France during the Great War, would often entertain the crowd

The steps leading up to the entrance to St Martin-in-the-Fields in 1941.

with tales of his times in Johannesburg, or when his father captained the Cambridge boat crew in 1856. His most famous story, however, was that of the British dud shell that had fallen through St Martin's roof and pierced the portico. It then bounced on the stone flags, missing a pillar, burst through the wood blocks on the street (causing a sizable hole) before jumping twelve feet in the air and coming to rest under the portico. 'What do you think of that?' he would cry, before the whole crypt joined in with 'Hip-hip for the shell.' Father McCormick died of heart failure in 1941, but he left behind a memory of all that represents the Blitz spirit.

On leaving St Martin's via its main entrance we are greeted with the famous view of Trafalgar Square. Ahead of you stands the National Gallery. During the war most of the paintings were stored underground in slate quarries and coal mines around Britain, guaranteeing their safety. The square itself was frequently the rallying point in both the First and Second World Wars for recruiting drives and raising money for war efforts. To this day each Christmas the people of Norway present a tree that is displayed here as a sign of gratitude for Britain's efforts on their behalf in the war.

Before ending this walk at Trafalgar Square underground station let us remember another day, VE day, when this was the scene of perhaps the biggest party ever thrown in the capital, with millions of flag-waving, dancing, singing people celebrating the victory. It was a moment many had dreamed of when sheltering during the Blitz or during the long-drawn-out periods of the blackout. In the words of the wartime hit song,

'*I'm going to get lit up when the lights go up in London,*
I'm going to get lit up like I've never lit before.
You will find me on the tiles, you will find me wreathed in smiles.
I'm going to get so lit up I'll be visible for miles.
The city will sit up when the lights go up in London.
It's going to get lit like the Strand, but only more, much more,
And before the parties played out, they'd have fetched the fire brigade out,
For the litist uppist scene you ever saw!' (viii)

(i) *A Prophet at Home* – Douglas Reed – Jonathan Cape 1941

(ii) *Private Diary* – Charles Graves – 1940 unpublished

(iii) *Carry on London!* – Ritchie Calder – English University Press 1941

(iv) *Hell Came to London* – Basil Woon – Peter Davies 1941

(v) *Hell Came to London* – Basil Woon – Peter Davies 1941

(vi) *Their Finest Hour* – Winston S Churchill – Cassell & Co 1949

(vii) *Bombers Moon* – Negley Farson – Victor Gollancz Ltd 1941

(viii) *I'm Going to Get Lit Up* – Alan Breeze & Billy Cotton's Band 1943

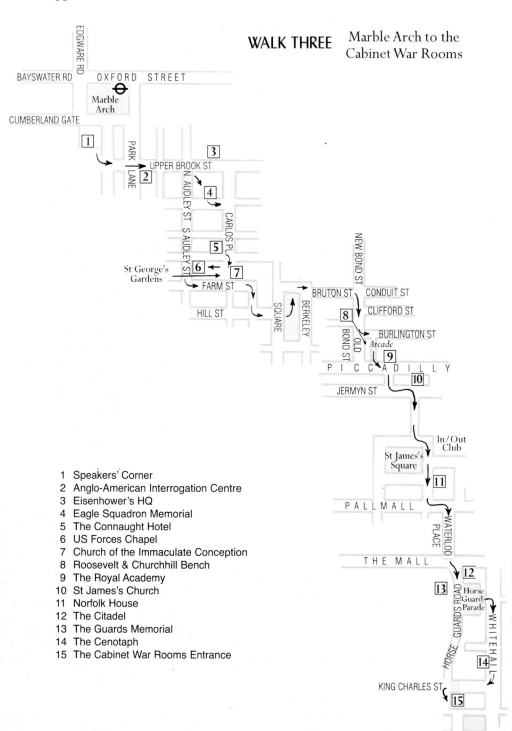

WALK THREE Marble Arch to the Cabinet War Rooms

1 Speakers' Corner
2 Anglo-American Interrogation Centre
3 Eisenhower's HQ
4 Eagle Squadron Memorial
5 The Connaught Hotel
6 US Forces Chapel
7 Church of the Immaculate Conception
8 Roosevelt & Churchhill Bench
9 The Royal Academy
10 St James's Church
11 Norfolk House
12 The Citadel
13 The Guards Memorial
14 The Cenotaph
15 The Cabinet War Rooms Entrance

WALK THREE

Marble Arch to the Cabinet War Rooms

*Starting Point – **Marble Arch Station** (Central Line)*
*Finish Point – **King Charles Street** (The Cabinet War Rooms)*

During the twentieth century the United States has certainly been one of Britain's most faithful allies and vice-versa. There is no doubt that their assistance and eventual participation in the Second World War had a huge impact not only on its outcome but also in the day-to-day life of ordinary Londoners. The following walk bears this out as we pass pubs in which American serviceman drank, buildings in which their senior officers made major decisions, parks they spent nights encamped in and memorials on which they are commemorated.

Our starting point is Marble Arch Underground Station on the Central Line. Make your way out via subway three and come up on to street level via exit four, Speakers' Corner. Looking north across Marble Arch itself you will see a number of cinema complexes similar to those that were here during the war. One of them, the Regal, once hosted the European premiere of John Wayne's *The Fighting Seabees*. This, in addition to marching bands and celebrities, was attended by thousands of U.S. servicemen, a welcome evening of entertainment and colour for the capital. The date was April 1944, a period of quiet before Hitler's terror weapons V1 and V2 rockets began landing on London's streets in-mid June.

Speakers' Corner, where a V1 rocket landed on 18 March 1945.

Speakers' Corner, the gravelled area of Hyde Park in front of you, is where opinions have been expressed by anyone who wants to and a place that has attracted both bemused tourists and curious locals since 1872. Chartists, the Reform League, May Day demonstrators and the Suffragettes have all gathered here during the last century or so. Originally, this was where the gallows of Tyburn were situated. Used since 1196 for public executions, by 1571 these state-of-the-art gallows were of a triangular shape enabling twenty-one people to be hung at once. The condemned would often arrive drunk and in many cases perform to the watching crowd, proclaiming their innocence or their alliegance to the cause for which they were dying. This free speech in the face of authority eventually led this spot being championed by Reformers as the place for all views to be expressed, so in the mid-nineteenth century it took its current form. Lenin supposedly once spoke here, but a more unwelcome visitor arrived during the rush hour on 18 March 1945 in the shape of a V1 flying bomb that reduced the area to a pile of rubble. This was one of the final acts of Hitler's flying bomb campaign, the last V1 landing in Datchworth, Hertfordshire, just ten days later, on 28 March.

Continue south in the park and notice the area to the right full of deck chairs. This part of the park is now frequently used to host large-scale open-air concerts. Both classical and rock music can be heard here by the world's most famous artists. In the war years, however, the only show to be seen was courtesy of General Pile's anti-aircraft batteries which filled

Anti-Aircraft batteries get the better of the Luftwaffe in 1943.

this open space in the heart of London. Muzzle flashes lit up the night sky with the continual crump of their 3.7 inch guns, each of which were capable of firing ten rounds a minute. The area came in for some heavy bombing, not only because of the batteries located within the park, but also because it fell within the outer fringes of the vitally important Luftwaffe target area of government buildings.

The heaviest raid in this area occurred on the night of 15 November 1940 when 358 aircraft reached London and dropped over 400 tonnes of high explosives on the capital, a high proportion of which fell between Hyde Park and Albert Bridge. As anti-aircraft tactics improved and the mass raids subsided, the balance of power shifted and, three years later, on 17 January 1943, after a lull of nearly fourteen months, seventy-five aircraft raided London, of which only thirty reached their target. In reply the batteries here fired over 11,000 anti-aircraft shells. In fact during January 1943 more people were killed by falling anti-aircraft shells than German bombs! Leonard Moseley provides an eyewitness account of this area during a raid:

> '*Many people have been killed by our shrapnel in the past few days. The warden begged people to go inside and on Wednesday, during the daylight raid, people were pushed into Marks and Spencer's in Oxford Street and made to stay there as the Hyde Park guns were in full cry. In the park itself the wardens were hastily opening up the trench shelters. A friend from our office was there airing a dog and when the warning sounded everyone scattered. She was in conversation with an old lady who refused to budge. The noise of the guns was really terrific and my friend, Mrs Winnal, was really frightened but she didn't care to leave the old lady alone. They were near Queen Victoria's statue. Poor old Queen, I wonder what she would have said if she had been alive.*' (i)

After a short while we leave the park via Brook Street Gate and, minding the traffic, cross Park Lane into Upper Brook Street. No 18A was the home of author P.G. Wodehouse's character The Right Hon Shipton-Bellinger, (5th Earl of Brangbolton). Wodehouse was interned in Germany during the war and a series of radio broadcasts he made to America in 1941 led to deep and lasting resentment in Britain. Despite their content being mainly humorous, he was branded a traitor and was unable to clear his name until 1955. He moved to the States and became a U.S. Citizen and, for many who grew up reading his books, his Knighthood in 1975 just weeks before his death aged 93 came too late. Also along this imposing row of town houses was located an Anglo-American interrogation centre. The upper floors of a number of the houses were converted into top-secret office space. Here German PoWs with specific skills were brought, as intelligence sources

Upper Brook Street, where, during the war, there was an Allied Interogation Centre.

started to learn of the planned V1 and V2 terror weapons. Working here at the time was an American, Stirling Ralph Ryser. He remembers the day after a raid thus:

'About 100 planes during a fire bomb raid dropped two kilo magnesium incendiary bombs. The target was very likely Grosvenor Square where the American European Theatre of Operations Headquarters was located but they missed and most fell around Marble Arch and Hyde Park doing little damage. Many bombs did not explode and burn. The next day when I came into work a number of the men had unthinkingly brought in numerous magnesium bombs for souvenirs. I was very upset as none of them had any training in handling dangerous explosive devices, so I made them take them out of the office and hand them in red-faced to the authorities.' (ii)

Continue on down Upper Brook Street until you reach Grosvenor Square, home of the American Embassy. It is a modern structure, often surrounded by armed police and quite out of keeping with the rest of the square. Such were the connections with this part of London and the United States that in wartime it was known as 'Eisenhowerplatz'. Outside the Embassy can be found a statue of President Eisenhower placed here in 1989. On the northern side of the square can be seen two plaques on the side of buildings; one says it was Eisenhower's Headquarters between June and November 1942 and next door at No 20 was the home of the aircraft manufacturer Sir Frederick Handley Page whose company provided the RAF with both the Hampden and Halifax aircraft during the Second World War. Enter the

An original Metropolitan Police phone in Grosvenor Square.

square and the large memorial ahead of you is to Franklin D. Roosevelt. This was erected in 1948 after 200,000 British citizens subscribed to its fund

A recent photograph of the house in Grosvenor Square in which General Eisenhower had his headquarters in the war.

in just twenty-four hours. Near the southern gate is a memorial commemorating the 'Eagle' squadrons. These were the idea of Charles Sweeney, a wealthy American businessman living in London during the Blitz. In the autumn of 1940 three squadrons were raised from American pilots who volunteered prior to their own country's involvement in the war. Often led by British officers with extensive combat experience, they formed 71, 121 and 133 Squadrons of the Royal Air Force. The memorial lists all those who

The Eagle Squadron Memorial in Grosvenor Square.

flew with these Squadrons in wartime. The garden itself was completely redesigned postwar following significant bomb damage, as this corner of W1 provided many targets for the Luftwaffe.

Leave via the south-east corner and turn right into Carlos Place. You are now in the heart of Mayfair, still the most sought-after area in London, just as it was in 1940. The people who lived here suffered and 'did their bit' as much as anyone during wartime. It was here that Basil Woon met two female ambulance drivers who hadn't been to bed for twenty-four hours:

'The brunette, before the war, was one of Mayfair's bright young things. Her life was a round of Ascot, Wimbledon, Goodwood and the smart night clubs. She went to all the garden parties at the palace and her photograph was in the Bystander *or the* Tatler *half a dozen times a year (these two journals have been forced to merge for the duration). The other girl when I knew her was a dancer in the floorshow at the Dorchester. She was an American. When I see them this morning they are in greasy overalls, their faces and hands grimy, their hair tucked anyhow under uniform caps, and they are gulping steamy coffee at a roadside stall, their eyes are sunken with fatigue and desperate tiredness shows in their every movement, but still they are sharing a joke.'* (iii)

At the corner of Carlos Place and Mount Street is the Connaught Hotel. It was here that the exiled Charles de Gaulle stayed during the war years. Eisenhower and other high-ranking Allied commanders also regularly frequented the restaurant. Today the same aura of grandeur prevails as you pass the doorman en route to the nearby entrance gateway to Mount Street Gardens. These gardens were laid out in the 1890s on the site of Oliver's Mount, the remains of a fort erected during the English Civil War. Resist the temptation to enter the Church ahead of you; it is visited in a short while. Instead follow the gardens to the right where they open up into a lovely courtyard. Set among the trees and shrubs are a number of benches that record the names of American visitors who have made this corner of London their own both in war and peace. Leave the park via the South Audley Street exit and turn left.

The first building is the Grosvenor Chapel. This has been here since 1730. During the war it was used by the American Forces, who worshipped here. An inscription to the left of the entrance records this. The church today plays an active role in the local community. Whenever I have passed by there has been a service, wedding or concert in progress, giving the building a genuine sense of life. Continue south past the premises of Thomas Goode & Co Ltd, suppliers of fine china, glass, silver, linens and antiques to the rich, royal and famous

The American Red Cross building in Charles Street in Mayfair.

The Connaught Hotel, with Mount Street in the background.

since 1827. Among the survivors of the Blitz that have become an unofficial hallmark for the company are the seven-foot-high ceramic elephants made by the Minton factory for the 1889 Paris Exhibition. These two priceless creatures have stood in the window for over a century.

When you reach South Street turn left and, after the school, you pass a small London pub, the Punch Bowl. It has stood here since 1750 and has long been the meeting place of local military men. During the war it was the haunt of American servicemen encamped in the surrounding area. Inside, the pub retains its eighteenth century feel. The Punch Bowl and the Farm House opposite are among the few buildings in this street that predate the war. Heavily damaged during the Blitz, many have been rebuilt.

Further up on the left is the Catholic Church of the Immaculate Conception. Its entrance was severely damaged by enemy air action and was redesigned by Adrian Gilbert Scott post-war. At the same time the stained glass windows at this end of the church were designed by the notable Irish artist Evie Hone. The long-term effects of bomb damage were not completely repaired until 1977. As you enter, the small crypt to the right of the door contains a number of interesting war memorials. One is to Major General Sir Luke O'Connor who worshipped here. He was awarded one of the first Army Victoria Crosses during the Crimean War at the Battle of the Alma. Nearby is a memorial to Henry De Courcy Ward. He was killed aboard HMS *Cressy*, which was sunk alongside HMS *Aboukir* and HMS *Hogue* in one of the most tragic naval incidents of the Great War on 22 September 1914.

On leaving the church turn left and follow Farm Street for a short while to its junction with Hill Street and turn left again until you reach our next stop, Berkeley Square. Enter the gardens via the gate opposite the house that once belonged to Clive of India. Find a bench and pause for a while. These gardens house the oldest trees in London, planted in 1789. They survived the war, but the iron railings did not, being removed in 1941 to assist the war effort. However, they were replaced post-war. In fact a lot of work was carried out during that time, including the removal of two large surface air-raid shelters that were situated here. The park itself had been used to house an American army unit in the build-up to the Normandy landings. The area suffered its fair share of incidents during the Blitz. On Friday 13 September 1940 a house at the north end of the square was completely destroyed and incendiaries from a 'bread basket' fell on a complex of flats on the south side, burning some of them out. These were the homes of many celebrities from the theatre and film world and William Sistrom, an American film producer living here at the time, describes the

Berkeley Square today. It was once a US Army Camp.

scene,

> ' *I'd gone to bed pretty tired and still don't know what awakened me. But I smelled burning, so I looked out of the window, and there was the glow of a fire. But I had though it was the Mayfair Hotel, so I went back to bed. A little later, however, the smell grew stronger, so I opened the door and found the whole place was full of smoke. Well, it seemed a good idea then to move, so I dressed and groped my way downstairs. There was a lot of firemen and exited people in their nightclothes cluttering up the place. I didn't know any shelter nearby (the ones in the park were yet to be built) so I went to one at the other end of Mount Street. I don't want a walk like that again! Early in the morning I went back to the square expecting to find my building a smoking ruin, but the fire had been put out and everything was normal, so I went back to bed again!' (iv)*

Before you leave the square a walk to the northern end reveals a number of interesting bench plaques that commemorate American servicemen who served here sixty years ago. The large house in the north-east corner

Bomb damage in Berkeley Square.

at No 27 served as an Officers' hospital during the Great War. Returning to the centre of the square we should not forget the famous musical connection with this leafy corner of London, Eric Maschwitz's classic wartime ballad 'A Nightingale Sang in Berkeley Square'. This song, *The Roosevelt and Churchill Bench in Old Bond Street.*

Walking the beat in Mayfair, 1941.

perhaps more than any other, conjures up images of wartime London.

On leaving via the northern gate take Bruton Street which heads towards Bond Street. This short road was not without incident itself. On 16 September 1940 the house on the corner with Bond Street was hit and reduced to little more than a smoking hole in the ground, the same stick of bombs falling back along the road you have just taken and knocking down walls and roofs in Berkeley Square. During the immediate rescue operation one of the Heavy Rescue Squad workers, Robert Rowley, aged 32, was killed trying to extract a victim from the rubble. He was awarded a posthumous Commendation for Civil Defence Bravery by the King. Today on the same spot is a premises selling Hermes products. Turn right into Bond Street heading south towards Piccadilly. After a short distance near the junction with Grafton Street is a delightful modern sculpture depicting Roosevelt and Churchill sitting together on a bench. This was erected on the fiftieth anniversary of the end of the war in 1995 and provides a nice spot to squeeze between them and reflect on what we have seen so far.

Continue south along Bond Street before crossing left into Burlington Gardens and immediate right into Burlington Arcade. This very smart Regency-period glassed walkway that leads out onto Piccadilly houses exclusive designer boutiques and antique jewellery shops. The area was constantly being raided, given its close proximity to government buildings, and on numerous occasions this arcade was damaged. One post-raid shopper described it thus:

'Coming down Cork Street, I see

Burlington Arcade after a raid.

where the fire was last night. The upper end of the Burlington Arcade, that gem of the Regency where I have so often shopped, is a mess of twisted steel, and its windows broken.' (v)

As more commercial premises became damaged and as glass windows were a rare commodity, the 'war window' became a frequent fixture of shop fronts. This was a painted wooden frontage with a

Open, bitter, but undismayed.

couple of small glass panes for shoppers to peer through and observe the stock. These were often decorated with slogans of a topical and witty nature such as, 'Our windows are small, but our stock is big' or the barbers who proclaimed 'Open as usual – close shaves a speciality'.

Still on patrol in the arcade can be found the top-hatted beadles who prevent people from running, singing, whistling or carrying excess baggage! These are traditionally made up from ex-servicemen and were originally recruited from the ranks of the 10th Hussars. Londoners in the winter of 1940 continued to view the bombings with a mixture of contempt and intrigue, generally going about their business as usual. Douglas Reed said:

'Above the Burlington Arcade a glow, like a splash of red ink, spread into the night from a fire in Bond Street, and the fire bells clanged in the distance. A piece of anti-aircraft shell smacked into the pavement and I bent to look at it.' (vi)

When you reach Piccadilly look right and you can see the Ritz Hotel. In wartime this was a haunt for the rich and famous which, like the Savoy, offered safe dining and music during a raid. It also became the retreat for a number of exiled European monarchs who had fled to London as war ravished their own countries. Perhaps the most famous wartime resident here was King Zog of Albania. He had escaped via Italy and France with a sizeable portion of his country's wealth in his luggage. With his proud head of red hair and waxed moustache, this eccentric-looking Royal lived up to his appearance. His six hefty bodyguards always escorted him. On his arrival at the Ritz a porter enquired if was there was anything of value in his trunks. 'Yes', came the reply, 'gold!' It was not uncommon for him to clear the Ritz's dining room for the exclusive use of his family as its thick concrete walls offered better protection than his third-floor suite during a raid.

Meanwhile, for the less influential, next door, at the corner of Green Park, was Green Park Underground Station. Think back to the two young female ambulance drivers we spoke of in Mayfair on 11 January 1940. Estelle Tidman, aged twenty-six, was a London Auxiliary Ambulance Driver when she met her death here responding to an incident in the shelter below.

Head east and just past Burlington Arcade can be found the imposing Burlington House. This was built in the 1660s and is the last surviving example of the noblemen's mansions that once stood on the north side of Piccadilly. In 1854 it was acquired by the Government and used to house the Royal Academy of Arts, the Society of Antiquaries, the Royal Astronomical Society and other such establishments. Enter its courtyard which boasts a modern water 'feature'. A canister carrying incendiary devices landed here in September 1940 but caused little damage. A few days later, however, a larger raid was to cause more damage and Basil Woon again provides us with a description of the scene:

'The stone walls of Burlington House that house the Royal Academy are chipped and scarred with its windows broken. Everywhere the glass which crunched under my feet last night has been swept up into tidy piles in the gutter.

'Hardly a whole pane of glass remains and against the blast of these big bombs, the criss-crossed strips of gummed paper are entirely useless. Not only windows are broken, but window frames are blown in.' (vii)

At either side of the entrance to the Academy are war memorials to the Great War that survived the Blitz. On the right the Artist Rifles are commemorated. This territorial unit which formed the 28th Battalion of the London Regiment, was used for the most part as an officers' training unit. By 1917, however, they were fighting as infantry in their own right with the 63rd Royal Naval Division and suffered heavily at Passchendaele. In all 2,003 of its men were killed during the Great War.

Bomb damage is still visible on the brickwork of Albany

On the left a memorial commemorates the members of the Royal Academy who lost their lives in the Great War. Among them was E.S. Carlos, an officer with the Buffs (East Kents) who was killed on 'The Bluff' at Ypres in 1917. From time to time examples of the work of this talented artist still come up for auction.

Leaving the Academy and joining Piccadilly once more, almost directly opposite is Fortnum and Mason. Purveyors of fine foods to the gentry since the mid- eighteenth century, its business was built on its ability to supply officers with supplies in the field of battle. They once famously delivered to Raymond Asquith of the Grenadier Guards a hamper up to the front line on the Somme in September 1916. Almost opposite, on the north side of Piccadilly, is Albany. It is said of these buildings that not a window remained intact. One resident was blown, complete with his bed, from his apartment, both landing unharmed on

Piccadilly. A closer inspection of the brickwork reveals a great deal of damage.

Our next destination is St James's Church. A pedestrian crossing leads us to a small courtyard often given over to a busy little market. To the right of the entrance a stone tablet records the wartime damage caused to this Wren church. Before entering the church itself go to the right, where there are a number of tablets. A wall plaque here commemorates the destruction of the church during a night raid on 14 October 1940. The fire damage is still visible on the building's exterior walls, as is the newer brickwork. Among the 170 civilians killed that night in London were both the verger and his wife, Charles and Edith Murray. They are further remembered on a stone tablet inside the church on one of the many memorials and plaques from both World Wars. Another recalls that the portrait painter Mary Beale was buried in the church crypt, but her tomb was destroyed by enemy bombing. The church itself was finally rebuilt in 1954 and its churchyard designated a garden of remembrance.

St James's Church, Piccadilly, after the night raid on 14 October 1940. Note the sign saying 'Still in use'.

On leaving via the south exit we emerge onto Jermyn Street, still full of exclusive gentlemen's outfitters and shirt makers. This street has been almost entirely rebuilt after its total destruction on the night of 16/17 April

1941. This massive raid, the heaviest yet on the capital, involved 685 aircraft dropping 890 tonnes of high explosive and over 150,000 incendiary bombs. The raid lasted from 2100hrs until after 0500 the next morning. Over 1,100 Londoners were killed and 2,200 seriously injured. In retaliation the anti-aircraft batteries set around the capital had fired over 5,700 shells, while the civil defences tackled the 2,200 fires that had been started, Jermyn Street being among the largest.

The raid had ominously been predicted by the infamous Lord Haw Haw, otherwise known as William Joyce. Following an RAF bombing of Berlin on 9 April, he announced 'There's going to be a bombing' on his Germany Calling radio broadcast. Among the casualties that night was the 3rd Earl of Kimberley. He was killed while staying at his London residence at 48 Jermyn Street.

Just off of Jermyn Street, in his flat in Duke's Court, 32 Duke Street, the

Jermyn Street today. It was almost totally destroyed in 1941.

talented jazz musician and heartthrob Al Bowlly became another casualty of that evening. He was in bed reading when the bomb fell. At the time he was perhaps the country's finest performer and is probably best remembered for his signature tune 'Buddy can you spare a dime?'

Turning right into Duke of York Street we find ourselves in St James's Square, surrounded by imposing company offices and gentlemen's clubs, among them the Naval & Military Club in the north-east corner of the square. Opposite, outside the railings, can be found a memorial to PC Yvonne Fletcher who was shot by terrorists while on duty outside the then Libyan Embassy on 17 April 1984, forty-one years to the day after this square and the rest of London were being subjected to its heaviest raid so far during the war. The blast damage is still evident on the frontage of No 33. Next door, at Norfolk House, were the Allied Forces Headquarters. From this building both Operation Torch, the liberation of North Africa, and Operation Overlord, the liberation of North-West Europe, were planned. A number of the surrounding buildings were taken over by staff of the various Army Groups and Corps taking part in these two massive operations. At the entrance to Norfolk House a couple of bronze plaques commemorate this building's place in history. Continue south and you will be in Pall Mall. Turn left and head towards Trafalgar Square.

Winston Churchill, who, on the evening of 14 October 1940, was on the cupola of the Annexe, provides a vivid description of Pall Mall in wartime:

> 'The night was clear and there was a wide view of London. It seemed that the greater part of Pall Mall was in flames. At least five fierce fires were burning, and others in St James's Street and Piccadilly, but Pall Mall was the vivid flame picture. Gradually the attack died down and presently the all clear sounded.' (viii)

What he had witnessed had been the destruction of, among other buildings in Pall Mall, the Carlton Club. His Chief Whip, Captain David Margesson, who lived there, was among the 250 occupants inside the premises when it was hit. The entire façade of the building was blown out into Pall Mall, flattening a number of vehicles parked outside. The smoking room ceiling collapsed on top of the many members sheltering inside. Amazingly, all of them crawled out from under the pile of dust and rubble and, despite injuries, there were no fatalities in the building. Given the high proportion of Tory membership at the Carlton Club, Labour Cabinet members remarked, 'The devil looks after his own!' On that evening's bombing 170 Londoners were killed and over 600 seriously wounded.

Follow Pall Mall as far as the pedestrian crossing that takes you over the road and into Waterloo Place. On the corner opposite at No 104 is the

Reform Club. Opened in 1841, it was from here that a Mr Phineas Fogg set out on his voyage 'Around the World in Eighty Days'. Next door but one, the Traveller's Club at No 106, was formed to reunite gentlemen who had travelled abroad. It had to be restored in the 1950s following heavy bomb damage. Also damaged and situated in Waterloo Place is the old United Services Club, now the Institute of Directors. Formed as early as 1815 by senior army officers, the current building dates from 1828. The Duke of Wellington's mounting block is still outside. At No 14 Waterloo Place there was a public shelter in the basement. Capable of housing sixty people at a time, it was for use during daytime business hours only.

There are a number of interesting statues lining this open space, and by observing the blast damage on the monuments to Scott of the Antarctic, Field Marshal Campbell and Edward VII it is possible to work out the exact position where a bomb fell, right where you stand now.

Take the flight of stairs at the end of Waterloo Place and you enter The Mall. Look right to see Buckingham Palace, covered on another walk. Left heads towards Admiralty Arch. A ceremonial gateway between Trafalgar Square and the Mall built in 1910 as part of the national monument to Queen Victoria, it formed part of the large Admiralty complex at the northern end of Whitehall.

These buildings were repeatedly hit during the Blitz and many still show signs of damage. This led in part to the construction in 1940 of the

Buckingham Palace, looking down the Mall.

Admiralty Citadel, the ivy-covered dark concrete structure you see before you, once well described by Harold Macmillan as that building that 'graces or defaces Horse Guards Parade'. Its immensely thick walls and thirty-foot-deep foundations meant it was safe even from a direct 1,000lb bomb strike. This ensured safe communications between the Admiralty and its fleet, even while under direct attack. Nicknamed by Londoners 'Lenin's Tomb', it stands today awkwardly alongside its more glamorous eighteenth century neighbours, but stand it does.

The courtyard that houses the famous Trooping of the Colour now comes into view. Head towards the impressive Guards Memorial to your front. The bronze soldiers, cast from captured German guns, stand as a silent monument to the efforts of all Guards units during the Great War.

An elderly wartime policeman on traffic duty outside Horse Guards Parade.

On its sides the detailed carved panels and the list of battle honours represent an A to Z of the four years' fighting on the Western Front. It also bears the scars of enemy air action from the last war. The courtyard itself housed its own barrage balloon, preventing low-level attacks, and belts of barbed wire and armed guards were evidence of the fear that spies and parachutists could breach naval security. As you cross towards the archway ahead to your right similar security today protects the rear of Downing Street, so access to the memorials on that side of the parade ground can be difficult. The older buildings such as the Old Admiralty, the Paymaster General's Office and Dover House, which houses the Scottish Office, were hit on numerous occasions during the war and a casual glance at their frontages reveals replaced brickwork and deep scars.

Passing through the archway and out into Whitehall itself, here you can watch the Changing of the Guard. Remember, as you watch this simple but impeccably smart ceremony, that the soldiers are not just for display but are equally at home fighting in arctic, jungle or desert conditions. Our army today, as always, is one we can be justly proud of. Entering

The Whitehall side of Horse Guards Parade just before the war.

Whitehall, cross to its east side, passing in the centre of the road a statue of Sir Douglas Haig astride his charger and facing towards the Cenotaph. Again bomb damage is visible on its plinth. As you walk west towards the Houses of Parliament you pass three modern military statues. They are of Field Marshal Slim in his full jungle regalia, followed by Field Marshal Alanbrooke, graced with the title 'Master of Strategy' and finally Field Marshal Montgomery, simply inscribed 'Monty'. It is worth remembering that all three of these deservedly lauded leaders were products of the often-criticized Haig's command during the Great War. In 1918 in particular all underwent an immense learning curve that led to many of the modern battle tactics used by Second War commanders.

Cross back to the west side of Whitehall, passing the entrance to Downing Street. Churchill described numbers 10 and 11 during the 1940s as being

> *'Two hundred and fifty years old, shaky and lightly built by the profiteering contractor whose name they bear!'*

Following the Munich Crisis shelters for the occupants had been constructed, in addition to reinforcing the garden-level ceilings with wooden timbers. While this was designed to withstand light bomb damage it could not provide effective protection against a direct hit, so during September 1940 arrangements were made to transfer Ministerial Headquarters to more suitable government accommodation in Storey's Gate, known as 'the Annexe'. While these new premises were being prepared Churchill harked back to his experiences during the Great War, describing life in Downing Street as being exciting: 'One might as well have been at a battalion headquarters in the line.'

One evening in October 1940 a number of bombs were heard to drop close to No 10, one landing in Horse Guards Parade. Churchill went to investigate and then realized that the house had been struck. The bomb had reduced the kitchen and pantry to dust. The underground Treasury shelter just fifty yards away had taken a direct hit and the three civil servants on Home Guard duty inside were killed instantly. This close shave for the Prime Minister confirmed that safer more permanent accommodation was required nearby and they are our next stop.

As you head further down Whitehall you pass the Cenotaph, Lutyens' tribute to the nation's 'glorious dead'. During the Armistice Parade here at 1100hrs on 11 November 1940, while the traditional two-minute silence was being kept the peace was shattered by the sirens heralding an air raid. In a typical display of British stoicism not a person moved until the reveille was sounded on the bugle and all made their way calmly to the nearest shelter.

The Cenotaph, silhouetted by incendiary bombs landing in Whitehall.

Next right takes us into King Charles Street. Follow this to its conclusion at Clive's Steps. This spot was struck by a direct hit on 26 September 1940, proving to be a close shave indeed for the nearby Cabinet War Rooms. This is our final stop and access is gained via the sandbagged entrance to the left of the stairs.

Open every day except 24 to 26 December between 1000 and 1800 (last admissions 1715rs) and with an adult admission fee of £5.70 at the time of writing (there are reductions), the Cabinet War Rooms give a fascinating and essential flavour to any London Blitz tour. Largely hidden from the public until 1981, there are currently plans to extend this already extensive labyrinth of secret wartime offices by another two-thirds. About two hours are required to see all that is now on display.

The rooms were conceived in 1938 and in fact staffed as early as September of that year during the Munich Crisis. When war was finally declared Chamberlain held a number of Cabinet meetings here, but it was not until May 1940 that the then Prime Minister Winston Churchill announced that 'this is the room from where I'll direct the war'.

Over the next six years the rooms were continually adapted, expanded and reinforced to counter the ever-increasing destructive powers of enemy bombs, until 16 August 1945 when the doors were locked for the last time. At the height of the Blitz the Cabinet, Chiefs of Staff for naval, air and ground forces, together with the advanced headquarters for home forces, were all squeezed into the basement of this building known simply as the New Public Offices in George Street.

On the outside of the building the protective slab of concrete built at this time acts as an apron around its lower walls and provides us with a clue to its underground activity. On entering, a very useful and easy-to-use audio guide provides you with a tour of the complex. The fixtures and fittings are original or contemporary matches, all of which add to a very atmospheric visit. The Cabinet Room itself is laid out to represent 1658hrs on 15 October 1940, with a meeting about to start at 1700 and the Royal Marine orderly busy shuffling papers in preparation. Remember what sort of night the Prime Minister had had on the 14th, being nearly bombed out of his own house. As you explore further and deeper into the complex there are some delightful reminders of life here during the war, such as weather boards informing staff what was going on at street level (windy meant more than just a gust of air!). Remember, no whistling. It was one of Churchill's pet hates!

One of the most intriguing exhibits in the corridor seems to be little more than a toilet door displaying an engaged sign. Staff were said to have believed this was the only proper toilet in the building and therefore reserved for the use of the Prime Minister himself. In fact, behind this door was a humble pre-war broom cupboard that from 1943 housed a secure and very secret 'Sigsaly' telephone line linking Churchill and Roosevelt direct. While this system was at the cutting edge of technology the eighty tons of equipment and thirty kilowatts of energy needed to operate it were too large to be housed here. Instead they were in the basement of Selfridge's in Oxford Street.

Security was essential for this complex to run efficiently and, as far as can be ascertained, the Germans were never aware of the existence of the rooms. On guard was a contingent of Royal Marines backed up by 'Rance's Guard', a small volunteer unit of ex-Grenadier Guardsmen, unfit for military service, named and raised by the ever-present Mr George Rance.

Fitting the sirens on the rooftops of Whitehall.

Officially the civilian representative of the Ministry of Works, he was also a very likeable and charismatic sergeant- major like figure. There were rifle racks located around the building to be used by any member of staff in an emergency.

The map room, BBC radio transmitting room (from where Churchill made some of his most famous broadcasts) and even the room where he would spend the occasional night are all on view before you emerge via a well-stocked shop.

This completes our third walk. If you retrace your steps up King Charles Street and turn right into Whitehall, at the end of the street you will see the entrance to the modern Westminster Underground Station linking you with the Jubilee, District and Circle lines.

(i) *London Under Fire – 1944* – Leonard Moseley

(ii) *Personal Memoirs* – unpublished – Stirling Ralph Ryser

(iii) *Hell Came to London* – Basil Woon – Peter Davies 1941

(iv) As above

(v) As above

(vi) *A Prophet at Home* – Douglas Reed – Jonathan Cape 1941

(vii) *Hell Came to London* – Basil Woon – Peter Davies 1941

(viii) *Their Finest Hour* – Winston S Churchill – Cassell & Co 1949

WALK FOUR   Hyde Park Corner to Westminster

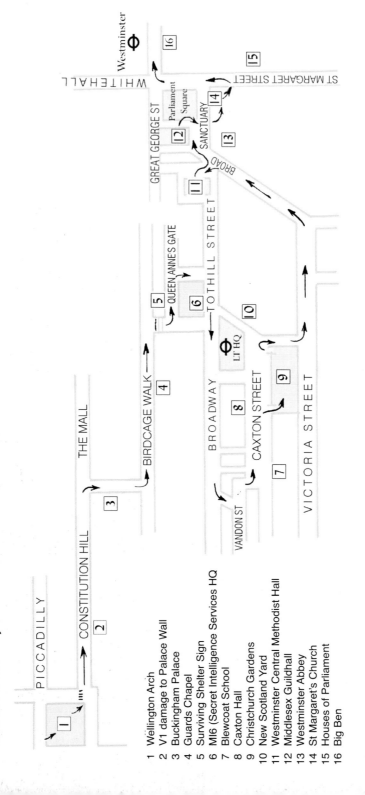

1 Wellington Arch
2 V1 damage to Palace Wall
3 Buckingham Palace
4 Guards Chapel
5 Surviving Shelter Sign
6 MI6 (Secret Intelligence Services HQ
7 Blewcoat School
8 Caxton Hall
9 Christchurch Gardens
10 New Scotland Yard
11 Westminster Central Methodist Hall
12 Middlesex Guildhall
13 Westminster Abbey
14 St Margaret's Church
15 Houses of Parliament
16 Big Ben

WALK FOUR

Hyde Park Corner to Westminster

*Starting Point – **Hyde Park Corner Station** (Piccadilly Line)*
*Finish Point – **Westminster Station** (District/Circle/Jubilee Lines)*

On arrival at Hyde Park Station, itself used as a public shelter during air raids, follow the signs for Exit 2. We start our walk in the large island that marks Hyde Park Corner. The subway walls are decorated with scenes depicting the life of the Duke of Wellington. If the Battle of Waterloo unfolds before your eyes then you are on the right track. At the final junction take the sign directing you to Green Park and you will emerge at street level safe from traffic.

Look west towards Knightsbridge and in front of you is one of the finest hotels in London, the Lanesborough. On its façade the name of St George's Hospital is still evident. In 1733 a Hospital Medical School was opened on this site. The current building was completed in 1844, with 350 beds for

Hyde Park Corner before the war.

The old St George's Hospital, now the Lanesborough Hotel, seen from the top of Wellington Arch.

patients. It closed as a hospital in 1980, St George's moving to various other premises in south-west London. During the Blitz it played an active role, being set aside to deal with wartime casualties. It escaped major damage when bombed in 1941. A 1,000 lb bomb fell on the lecture theatre, but failed to detonate. On the night of 10/11 May 1941 the hospital did blood transfusions for almost thirty hours non-stop. Many of the victims came from the nearby Alexandra Hotel, which had collapsed after taking a direct hit. Among the casualties was Police Constable John Dickie, wounded in the side by flying shell splinters. His lungs, diaphragm and spleen were ruptured. That night in the operating theatre medical history was made when the first transpleural splenectomy was successfully performed, despite the continuing air raid outside.

One of the most impressive of all the capital's war memorials is on the island in front of the Lanesborough – C.Sargeant Jagger's memorial to the men of the Royal Artillery killed between 1914 and 1918. Jagger, who was awarded the Military Cross during the Great War, includes vividly descriptive carved panels around its base, depicting various aspects of a gunner's life. An extension to the memorial was added by way of bronze panels commemorating the nearly 30,000 dead of the Royal Artillery in the

Second World War, some of them anti-aircraft gunners operating from the nearby Hyde Park batteries.

Following the view clockwise you will see a memorial to the Duke of Wellington himself, flanked by soldiers of England, Scotland, Ireland and Wales. Behind it is Apsley House, still in part the London home of the current Wellesley family. Once the home of the Iron Duke, it is often referred to simply as No 1 London, due to its close proximity to the old London Toll House. It now houses a museum in honour of the Duke of Wellington and is open between 1100 and 1700hrs daily with an entrance fee of £4.50, except on 'Waterloo Day', 15 June, when it is free. One further memorial on the island is that to the memory of the Machine Gun Corps, a bronze figure depicting David holding Goliath's sword surmounted by two Vickers heavy machine guns. This has long been the subject of controversy over its inscription: 'Saul hath slain his thousands and David his ten thousands'.

The sculptor, F. Derwent Wood, had not seen service in the Great War and it makes a fascinating contrast to Jagger's work nearby.

A peculiar wartime feature next to the Wellington Arch was a huge mound of earth, spoil from primitive shelter trenches dug in Hyde Park at

the time of the Munich Crisis. Policemen stationed at the Arch had planted this vast bank with Alpine plants that by 1944 were set to match the slopes of the Matterhorn!

Our next stop is the large and imposing Wellington Arch, built in the 1820s. A huge statue of Wellington astride his charger once sat on top, but many Victorians, including the Queen, commented unfavourably about its size and the Duke was removed to Aldershot garrison in 1885. From the 1930s the rooms inside the Arch housed a small police station and during the war it became the local reporting/control centre. An air raid siren was put on the sculpture of 'Peace descending into the quadriga of war'. The building suffered only slight shrapnel damage as a result of enemy air action. Late one evening in autumn 1944 Robert Henrey was invited

A policeman stands watch over London, 1940.

up on to the roof by PC Kingsley Elliot stationed there at the time:

'From this height one sees the queer collection of huts built on the rooftop of St George's Hospital, looking like a superimposed settlement. The police of Wellington Arch know every inch of that hospital, for they have brought many a street casualty there, the iconic pillars of the Duke of Wellington's monstrous mansion with its flagpost knocked askew by the bomb which sliced out a couple of houses from the aristocratic row in which the present King and Queen lived when they were the Duke and Duchess of York!' (i)

Thanks to English Heritage this famous London landmark, once the scene of an assassination attempt on the King, has been saved from its recent state of disrepair and is now open to the public for a modest charge of £2.50. Opening times are seasonal, so it is advisable to arrive between 1000 and 1600hrs between Wednesday and Sundays. Once in, allow the best part of an hour to view the museum, set on various floors that lead eventually up to the rooftop gallery. This provides an excellent 'firewatchers' view'

The air-raid siren on the quadriga on top of the Wellington Arch.

over central London. To stand here looking out above the roofs of the buildings is worth the entrance fee alone.

Leave Wellington Arch and head via the subway or pedestrian crossing to Constitution Hill. Before then, stop. Basil Woon describes this spot the morning after a raid in September 1940:

'Hyde Park Corner received a humdinger just inside the park gates, making a large crater which the limousines are carefully skirting this morning. About a hundred yards away in Piccadilly, one of those extremely massive-looking mansions, apparently built of stone, stands now sadly revealed as only a brick house camouflaged with stone in front. But neither the King's former home nor Wellington House are damaged.' (ii)

The house he describes was No 145 Piccadilly. Now a modern hotel marks the spot.

The entrance to Constitution Hill is now via a new memorial. The gates commemorate the efforts of the volunteers from Africa, the Sub-Continent and the Caribbean in the last two wars. Opened in the spring of 2002 this overdue memorial is inscribed with the words 'Our future is greater than

The north wall of the gardens of Buckingham Palace. New brickwork and a tilted lamppost show where the V1 exploded.

our past'. It is often forgotten that over some 4,500,000 men from these countries fought alongside Britain in the two world wars. Continuing south, the wall on the right of the road belongs to Buckingham Palace. After a short while the colour of the brickwork changes and a new stretch of wall is evident. This shows the damage from a flying bomb that landed on this spot just after midnight on Tuesday 20 June 1944. The following Sunday another landed in the grounds of the Palace, though little damage was caused.

Continue, with Green Park on your left, and you soon pass a granite water feature that is a memorial commemorating Canadian efforts in both wars. On your right the more familiar sight of Buckingham Palace comes into view. This spot at the west end of the Mall is always busy with tourists, especially at the time of Changing the Guard. Cross in front of the Palace. It was bombed for the first time just a week into the Blitz on 13 September when a stick of six bombs were dropped in or around the grounds. None of the Royal Family was injured though both the King and Queen were in residence at the time. Two bombs landed in the Quadrangle, two just outside the entrance where you are now, one in the rear garden and the last hit the chapel, causing great damage. One eyewitness who was walking through St James's Park when a twin-engined raider flew overhead, well below the level of the barrage balloons, described the incident:

'He cut out his engine and when he was about 2,500 feet up and over the lake I heard the whistle of bombs. I threw myself down under a tree and happened to be gazing directly at the Palace as the bombs exploded. It looked at first as if the whole building had gone skyward. Bits of masonry were tossed hundreds of feet into the air. There was a cloud of dirt and what looked like smoke obscuring the front of the Palace, but when it settled I could see the building was still there. I ran back and found the earth just settling down in a huge crater right in front of the main gates. A soldier was on his back being attended to by another. I went through the gates and saw another crater in front of the Quadrangle. All the Palace windows within eyesight had been smashed. Debris was everywhere.' (iii)

The rebuilt north lodge of Buckingham Palace. Its predecessor was destroyed in 1941.

The raid had taken place just after 1100 hours. While this was no doubt a daring attack by a lone German aircraft, it had a very positive impact on London's morale. Only two staff had been slightly wounded and now the King and Queen were at one with the people. As the Queen herself was reported to have said, 'I'm glad we've been bombed. It makes me feel I can look the East End in the face'.

On the next occasion that the Palace was damaged the King and Queen were not in residence. On Saturday 8 March 1941 London received its first major raid for almost two months. The Palace's North Lodge took a direct hit and an on-duty policeman, Stephen Robertson, was wounded in the blast. Later that day, at Charing Cross Hospital, he died of his wounds.

Leaving the Palace, head south to Birdcage Walk and turn left, our next stop being Wellington Barracks. On the Barrack Railings close to the Guards shop is a bronze plaque commemorating an Australian Victoria Cross holder, Gunner Arthur Sullivan. In August 1919 in North Russia he rescued four of his colleagues who had fallen into a river while his unit was fighting a rearguard action. The enemy was less than a hundred yards away. On 9 April 1937, as part of the Coronation celebrations, Gunner Sullivan was one of a number of Victoria Cross winners lined up on the road outside Wellington Barracks. A traffic accident occurred near this spot and he died of head wounds, so his comrades erected this plaque.

Wellington Barracks offers an impressive backdrop to Birdcage Walk.

Soon you will see a small scout car. Go in here and to your right is the entrance to the Guards Museum. This traces the long and glorious history of the foot guards and, for a £2.50 entrance fee, it is recommended to those with a more general interest in military history. Just inside the entrance is a small case with a number of Blitz artefacts.

For those with less time available make for the Guards' Chapel opposite. The original building was put up in 1838. At 11:20 on Sunday 18 June 1944 a V1 flying bomb made a direct hit on the building, Lieutenant Colonel Lord Edward Hay of the Grenadier Guards had just finished reading the lesson when it struck. He was killed at the lectern. The congregation had heard the bomb flying overhead, then the engine cut out and a few seconds silence before the wailing of the bomb's descent. The roof, upper walls, stone pillars and west door portico all came down in the blast. Within seconds 119 soldiers and civilians out of the congregation of 180 were dead. This was the worst flying bomb incident of the war.

The Guards' Chapel in June 1944 after the dèbris had been cleared up.

Debris was piled ten feet high, blocking the entrance, and eyewitnesses described the total stillness of the scene. One of the lucky few, the Bishop of Maidstone, had been waiting in the sanctuary to preach when the bomb struck and escaped injury. Almost immediately the rescue operation began and teams worked continuously forty-eight hours. Among those who could not be saved were the Commanding Officer of the Scots Guards, Lieutenant Colonel John Cobbold, and Major James Causley Windram, the Household Division's Director of Music.

Lady Gordon Lennox, whose husband, Bernard Charles, was killed in 1914 while serving with the Grenadier Guards near Ypres and is buried in Zillebeke Churchyard, had perhaps come to remember her lost husband and pray for her son George, at this time in Italy commanding the 5th Battalion Grenadier Guards, when she was killed in the church. Her son survived the war, being awarded the DSO and rising to the rank of Lieutenant General.

When the rubble was finally cleared the continuation of services was high on the agenda, almost as an act of defiance. A Romney Hut was erected and the doors were opened again as a place of worship on Christmas Day 1944. The building you see today was completed in 1963. In its foundations are the remains of over two thousand war memorials that used to deck the walls of the chapel but were destroyed beyond repair. They are today listed on the back walls. Inside, the tragic events on June 1944 are commemorated in the form of a roll of honour and numerous private memorials, including that to Captain Douglas Hall of the Canadian Grenadier Guards who was visiting that Sunday. Three maple trees have been planted in the grounds to commemorate Lieutenant Harold Dodds of the Scots Guards who was also in the congregation that day. The impressive golden East Portico is the one of the few remaining features from the original building.

On leaving the chapel return to Birdcage Walk. Opposite you is St James's Park. This was one the principal recreation areas for locals during the war. Teenager Marie Berry describes the park in wartime:

> *'But my deepest appreciation of that lovely little park was felt in the night hours, when, its gates left open for ease in dealing with incendiary bombs, with a companion or two, or better still alone, I would slip out of the heat and bustle of the shelter for a quiet space under the stars, and even Jerry, buzzing ominously in the distance, could not steal that sense of peace which out of doors on a summers night can give.'* (iv)

Turn right and after a short while you reach the entrance to Queen Anne's Gate, a perfect corner of Georgian London, whose mansions are still adorned with boot scrapers and torch snuffers. Turn right and at No 28 a

The statue of Queen Anne which was bricked up during the war.

The 'shelter' sign on the wall of 28 Queen Anne's Gate still visible after 60 years.

painted symbol denoting an air raid shelter is still visible on the wall. Further down is the statue of Queen Anne. During the war this was protected by a brick wall canopy, remains of which are still visible. Both the shelter and the brick shield around the queen were well placed when you look at the amount of scarring on the facades of these buildings. At No 1 Sir Edward Grey, the Foreign Secretary during the Great War, lived, famous for his statement 'The lamps are going out all over Europe. We shall not see them lit again in our lifetime'. His time here is marked by a blue Heritage plaque. Walk south down Carteret Street onto Broadway and in front of you is the imposing London Transport Headquarters at No 55. Built in the late 1920s and bedecked with sculptures by Eric Gill, Henry Moore and Jacob Epstein among others, its fourteen storeys tower above St James's Park underground station. The premises had its own roof spotters and fire section to deal with the not infrequent incidents that occurred here and they prevented the building from being severely damaged. On 10 May 1941 a number of incendiary devices were dealt with but not before telephone lines and lighting had been taken out.

No.54 Broadway, wartime headquarters of the Secret Service.

The Blewcoat School today.

Opposite, at No 54, now housing a number of modern business offices, was the Headquarters of the Secret Intelligence Services. Also known as MI6, they were based here between 1924 and 1966. On the third floor were the offices of Dr R.V. Jones, of the Air Ministry Department for Scientific Intelligence. It was from here that both the 'Knickebein' and 'X Gerat' Luftwaffe target-finding systems were discovered and counter-measured.

Continue into Petty France past the modern Home Office complex and then left into Vandon Passage. The buildings all appear to be of 1930s vintage and presumably have survived the Blitz intact. At Vandon Street go round to your left and past the entrance to an old London Transport Garage. The original markers are still visible in front of the doors. It is used for private parking now. In front of you is the brick-built Blewcoat School on Caxton Street. This small school was opened in 1709 for the education of poor children and it remained as such until 1920 when the National Trust took it over and ran a shop just as exists today. During the war years, however, it was commandeered by the military and by 1944 was used by

Graffiti left by American soldiers when they occupied the Blewcoat School.

the United States Army as a warehouse in the lead-up to D-Day. Outside on the western doorway can be seen both the bayonet scrapings left by bored sentries and some graffiti left by GIs. On leaving, head east down Caxton Street. On your left is Caxton Hall. This grand old building was once Westminster Town Hall and many politicians have addressed crowds from here. In the last war some of Churchill's speeches were given from here and an ageing plaque makes mention of this. Today it is covered in scaffolding and its future is uncertain. Further along Caxton Street is the entrance to St Ermin's Hotel. Now, as in wartime, it proves popular with American visitors. During the war some floors were turned into government offices, though their true purpose is still classified. The close proximity to the SIS offices in Broadway may not be a coincidence. Almost opposite Caxton Hall is the entrance to a small park, Christchurch Gardens, located on the site of a thirteenth-century church of the same name. Oliver Cromwell's men used the original building at one stage as a stable. Later it became a military prison for Scots captured at the Battle of Worcester, many of them dying in the terrible conditions that prevailed. A new church was built in 1843 known as Christ Church, Broadway. On 17 April 1941 a number of incendiary bombs fell in the area of the gardens, and the church roof caught fire. The joint efforts of the fire services, civil defence and local people failed to control the blaze and the building was destroyed. By morning only the tower survived. In 1954, to make way for a new telephone exchange, the tower and adjoining vicarage were pulled down. Today it provides a quiet spot for people to eat their lunch and only a solitary headstone set into the pavement as you enter from Caxton Street

A typical post-blitz scene. Many buildings in Victoria Street were destroyed.

Scotland Yard prepares for war. Victoria Embankment, 1939.

reminds you of its past.

Leaving the gardens, the busy road ahead of you is Victoria Street which leads from Victoria Station in the west to Westminster Abbey in the east. Head towards Westminster Abbey and note the relatively few pre-war buildings that have survived in this area – a solitary pub, the Albert, and Artillery Mansions which provided wartime 'service flats' for overseas journalists. On your left is New Scotland Yard which opened in 1967. Wartime headquarters for the Metropolitan Police were on Victoria Embankment opposite Cannon Row Police Station. The modern building is perhaps most famous for its revolving sign that spins 14,000 times daily and can be seen on the Broadway entrance.

Continue down Victoria Street and a number of famous London landmarks come into view. Our next stop is the large domed building at the junction with Storey's Gate, Westminster Central Methodist Hall. It was built between 1905 and 1911 to a grand Edwardian standard and many of the world's leaders have spoken here. The auditorium seats over 2,000 people and still doubles as an active church. The inaugural assembly of the United Nations took place here in 1946, mainly due to the fact that the building survived the war almost entirely intact and provided the perfect venue for such an occasion. It is the building's wartime history that is of interest to us, so enter the impressive lobby and stairwell and make your way down a floor to the area that now acts as a cafeteria.

Here was the largest public shelter in the Westminster area. It acted as such for a total of 1,832 days. Separated into five separate sections by low sandbagged dividing walls, a nurse, hot soup and bread, entertainment and later bedding were provided for hundreds of people during air raids. Section five, for casual shelterers, provided striped deck chairs and became known locally as 'the Promenade'. In 1941 the council built specific blast walls replacing the sandbags and the gent's toilet was equipped with a dartboard and made available to gentleman smokers, welcome indeed as the shelter had since its inception been a No Smoking area. All this led to

Bomb damage at Westminster, while the inhabitants took shelter in the Central Methodist Hall.

a regular subterranean community building up under the watchful eyes of the Reverend Doctor Sangster and his wife. A local Chelsea artist was among the shelterers and before long three excellent reproductions of Pinkie, The Blue Boy and The Laughing Cavalier adorned the walls. While the shelter itself did not take a direct hit, the area surrounding it suffered greatly. During the heavier raids Dr Sangster would hold short services, often interrupted by explosions and someone remarking, 'There goes Victoria Street' or 'They got the hospital again'.

An unknown shelterer left this description in 1941:

> *'One particular night it was very bad. Reports came in that the whole of London was ablaze. My father, who at that time was one of the fire pickets on top of the dome of Central Hall, said it was one of the most frightening things he has ever seen. We were like an island with fire all around us, but we came through unscathed.'*(v)

On leaving the cafeteria level go up to reception. Tours are available free of charge most weekdays, a guide will take you into the great hall and give a good general history of the building, most of which was commandeered by the armed forces during the war. It was not unusual, however, for important government meetings to take place in the great hall itself.

Higher up (and open to the public during London's Open House days) at the top of the dome is a fantastic view over London. It was from here that fire watchers stood guard, ready to report incidents to the ARP control centre and to deal with fires caused by incendiaries to the dome itself. Many have left their mark by scratching their names into the soft lead shell.

On leaving Central Hall pass across the front of the modern Queen Elizabeth II Banqueting Centre and around the front of the medieval-looking Middlesex Guildhall. It was in fact built in 1913 and in wartime was a military court. Today it still acts as a criminal court. Inside the foyer can be found a plaque making mention of the building's wartime activities and a display case containing items of militaria and a memorial to the Westminster Rifles. Alas access is only granted to the accused or witnesses, which seems a shame, but no doubt necessary in the security-heightened environment that prevails today.

Cross over Broad Sanctuary towards the Abbey itself. Despite appearing intact today, the Abbey perhaps suffered more wartime damage than any other building in this area. Pre-war war steps for its protection had been implemented, all the staff had taken a fire-fighting course and extensive fire-fighting equipment had been bought. 60,000 sandbags had been piled high to protect windows, doorways and immovable statues; smaller statues and works of art had been hidden away in the Aldwych tunnel for the duration of the war. In the pews were cards telling worshippers what action to take in the event of an air raid: 'Shelter can be found in the crypt of the Central Methodist Hall and the choir will lead the way with all due reverent haste'. Fire watchers and staff were provided with a purpose-built shelter in the nearby college gardens and an arrangement was made with the local fire services that the Abbey would take priority if an incident occurred, given its religious and historical importance.

During the opening months of the bombing all seemed to be working to plan. The west window suffered slight damage in September 1940 and the Henry VII Chapel had its windows blown out when a bomb landed nearby, damaging the Houses of Parliament. These incidents, and another in October when the Little Cloisters were struck, were dealt with successfully by the Abbey's trained fire-watching staff. No amount of training, however, could have helped them with what was to occur on the night of 10 May 1941.

The moon was full, coinciding with an extremely low ebb tide on the Thames. Over 507 Nazi bombers carrying 711 tons of high explosives and over 86,000 incendiary bombs rained fire on the capital from 2300 to 0530 hrs. 1,436 Londoners were killed and 1,800 injured in what turned out to

Damage to Westminster Abbey sustained during the raid of 10 May 1941.

be the heaviest and most costly raid on London of the war. On the Abbey, a single incendiary fell and lodged itself just out of reach in the central lantern roof. Soon the roof was ringed with flames and came crashing down onto the flagstones some 130 feet below.

Though it eventually burnt itself out, this incident demanded the energy of most of the staff, while further incendiaries took root in the roofs of surrounding church buildings, melting lead and burning houses. By the morning, when the all clear sounded, onlookers surveyed a scene of scorched devastation. All were amazed to see a pair of rare Black Redstarts who had made their nest in the ruins.

There are a number of memorials in the Abbey itself connected with the last war, including an RAF chapel, a small Nurses Chapel, accessible only by request, and, of course, the tomb of the unknown warrior. Entrance is £6.00 between 0900 and 1645hrs Monday to Friday and 0900 to 1445hrs on Saturday.

A full afternoon is needed to do justice to this, one of the nation's treasures, and the Abbey can get crowded, with frequent queuing.

If time does not allow a visit to Westminster Abbey an essential stop on

St Margaret's Westminster.

this walk is the smaller, quieter church of St Margaret's, set in the Abbey grounds. The entrance is to the North of the Abbey itself and there is no fee. St Margaret's somehow manages to retain the feel of a country church despite its urban location. Indeed, it still acts as the parish church for the House of Commons.

A place of worship has existed here since the latter half of the twelfth century, the current building dating from 1523. The grass area outside the entrance is used as a Field of Remembrance every November when small poppy crosses are laid to remember the war dead. In 1940 this custom was dedicated to the soldiers on the Home Front, remembering members of the Civil Defence and civilians killed in the bombings. The church itself suffered a fair amount of damage during the Blitz and some of this is still evident. The most simple, yet evocative, Blitz memory is to be found on the eastern end of Pew 38, still scorched with fire damage. Sit here for a while and look to your left. The stained glass windows have been replaced in part with clear panels. The originals were destroyed when an oil bomb came through the north aisle. Worst effected, however, was the memorial to the Reverend James Palmer nearby which is forever blackened. Also destroyed was a memorial to Wenceslaus Hollar who is buried in the churchyard. He is today commemorated by a modern oval memorial on the same spot. The impressive east window which commemorates the marriage of Arthur, son of Henry VII, to Catherine of Aragon was removed for safekeeping to Putney during the war, thereby preserving it. The windows on the southern aisle remained and were completely destroyed. The present ones were designed by John Piper and record the demise of the originals. On leaving by the smaller door near to a memorial to Sir Walter Raleigh, executed not far from here, the Palace of Westminster comes into view. Turn right and walk past the back of Westminster Abbey. The exterior walls are clearly shrapnel-damaged. This is the outside of the small RAF chapel. A keen eye will spot the hole caused by a fragment of a

Shrapnel damage to the exterior of Westminster Abbey.

German bomb which landed near here. In fact it dropped behind you on the night of 27 September 1940, landing between Richard the Lionheart and the House of Commons itself. Cross over. King Richard had the rear of his horse blown away and his sword was famously bent. This has since been repaired. The windows behind were blown in and after the war replaced with stained-glass coats of arms of all members and staff who died in the Second World War.

While all parts of the Palace of Westminster were damaged, the House of Commons suffered the most, the building being almost entirely rebuilt following the heavy raids of May 1941. On arriving for work the day following an attack Winston Churchill's private secretary said, 'After no previous raid has London looked so wounded next day.'

During the raid on 10/11 May 1941 a fire started in the rafters of Westminster Hall. This quickly spread to the Members' Lobby, the roof of

Blast damage to the House of Commons.

Restored House of Commons in 2002.

which collapsed. Only days earlier a vote of confidence over Churchill's leadership had taken place in the very spot that was now a heap of smouldering girders and masonry. Throughout the war, in the relative safety of a vault beneath the Central Lobby, important war work of a different kind took place, in the form of a factory hastily constructed to assemble precision instruments for aircraft. This was manned by various members of staff from the Houses of Parliament, an idea that was repeated by many public and private establishments around the country.

Giles Gilbert Scott designed the new house, finally completed and ready for sittings by October 1950. The entrance to the Members' lobby is known as the Churchill Arch and is made from rubble from the original building. Not all the raids on the Palace of Westminster wreaked such havoc, however. Basil Woon described the aftermath of 14 September 1940:

'An incendiary bomb fell on the roof of the House of Lords last night,

penetrated to a washroom, and was put out. There is no great harm done. (It will I fear take more than an incendiary bomb to destroy the House of Lords. However, its capacity for mischief is greatly reduced during the war, for most of its members are, of course, either in their country homes or in uniform, and a bare handful attend the debates).' (vi)

As you walk round the outside of the Palace, Parliament Square is behind you again. This area was a mass of barbed-wired entanglements during the Blitz, on account of fears of enemy parachutists. The Westminster Home Guard, mostly made up of Members of Parliament and staff, built an ingenious concrete pillbox in the centre of the square that from a distance resembled a W.H. Smith's newsagents. Today the statue of Churchill, unveiled in 1973, stands nearby. The spot was supposedly chosen by Sir Winston himself, though he had reservations about becoming encrusted with bird droppings. Thankfully, he appears clean today.

A totally gutted House of Commons, 1942.

Turning the corner into Bridge Street we see the entrance to Westminster Hall, the oldest remaining structure in the Palace of Westminster complex. The roof beams are made from 600-year-old Hampshire Oak. Amazingly, these survived a direct hit in May 1941. The traditional use of Westminster Hall has been for state ceremonies and occasional courts of law or trials. It was here that 300,000 mourners passed the coffin of Winston Churchill as he lay in state in 1965. Not unlike the lying-in-state of the Queen Mother in 2001.

During the night of 10/11 May 1941 firefighters were fortunately on the scene when the roof of the great hall was set alight. The doors to the hall were locked from the inside, so, after quick consultation with a member of parliament who had just arrived from his nearby home, the ancient oak doors were smashed open by firemen's axes and, once inside, nearly fifty pumps tackled the blaze in the rafters. High flagstone walls meant that after a short while crews were nearly waist-high in water. Falling masonry and timbers made this a hazardous task for the firemen:

> *'Remember the building is a thousand years old, it must be saved. The firemen were in no mood for a history lesson. Sub Officer Joe Edmunds growled – Never mind if it is a thousand years old, don't risk your bloody necks if its gets dangerous.'* (vii)

Local water supplies were soon exhausted so the nearby Thames was utilized by dragging a trailer pump down the steps of Westminster Pier. After an hour or so the fire appeared under control. As Fireman Saunders was relieved by an oncoming crew he recalled, ' a chunk of Big Ben landing at his feet, but he cheered up when the old clock boomed the half hour'.

Ahead of you is the 'old clock', perhaps London's most famous landmark, the 316-foot-high tower of Big Ben. Officially known as St Stephen's Tower, it was decided when Parliament was rebuilt in 1841 that a tower containing a bell to chime hourly should be included.

The bell, weighing over 13 tons, was first heard across London in 1858 and a special session in Parliament was held that afternoon to name it. During the lengthy debate Sir Benjamin Hill, the Chief Lord of Woods and Forests, affectionately known to his colleagues as 'Big Ben', rose and spoke on the issue for what seemed an eternity. When he finally sat down a voice from the benches shouted, 'Why not call it Big Ben and be done with it?' When the laughter died down the fate of the great bell of Westminster had been decided.

The chimes, synonymous with London, became a sound of comfort and reassurance both at home and abroad via the BBC's broadcasts during the long nights of the Blitz. Its precise timekeeping, even during air raids, seemed to say 'London can take it' during the darkest hours. Big Ben survived a dozen hits of various degrees; masonry was chipped, the glass in the clock face was blown out but the clock still chimed. On the night of 10 May 1941, when the rest of the Palace of Westminster was facing destruction, it did lose half a second's time, but it continued to strike. Amazingly, all the efforts of the Luftwaffe could not achieve as much as a flock of starlings who, in 1949, perched on one of the clock's long hands and slowed it by four and half minutes.

You are now approaching Westminster Bridge. During the war a temporary bridge was built alongside this one in case of emergencies, but all traces of it have gone today. To ease congestion due to bomb-torn roads the River Thames was once again used to its full potential with a regular taxi service operating between Greenwich and Westminster. Londoners could argue that such a service would be helpful today. You are now opposite the entrance to Westminster Underground Station where in wartime a Lyons Tea Room stood. This marks the end of our walk.

(i) – *The Siege of London* – Robert Henrey – Temple Press 1946

(ii) – *Hell Came to London* – Basil Woon – Peter Davies 1941

(iii) – As above

(iv) – *A Thousand & One Nights* – Marie Berry (private publication)

(v) – *Life in the Shelter* – Private Publication

(vi) – *Hell Came to London* – Basil Woon – Peter Davies 1941

(vii) – *The City that Wouldn't Die* – Richard Collier – Collins 1959

A wartime view of Big Ben.

WALK FIVE London Bridge to St Paul's

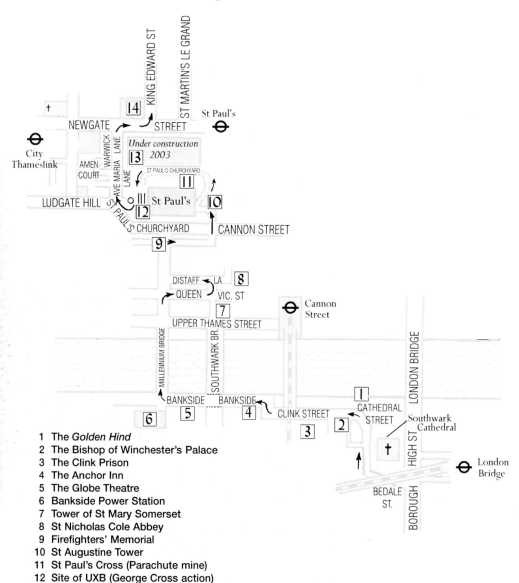

1 The *Golden Hind*
2 The Bishop of Winchester's Palace
3 The Clink Prison
4 The Anchor Inn
5 The Globe Theatre
6 Bankside Power Station
7 Tower of St Mary Somerset
8 St Nicholas Cole Abbey
9 Firefighters' Memorial
10 St Augustine Tower
11 St Paul's Cross (Parachute mine)
12 Site of UXB (George Cross action)
13 Paternoster Square
14 Christchurch Memorial Garden

WALK FIVE

London Bridge to St Paul's

*Start Point – **London Bridge Station** (Terminus/Northern Line)*
*Finish Point – **St Paul's Underground Station** (Northern Line)*

Our final walk begins where Walk One finished at London Bridge Station. Follow the signs to Borough High Street North and, emerging at street level, head towards the river until you reach the junction with Bedale Street. After a few days' respite 14 February 1941 brought the first enemy aircraft over the city since the night of the 3rd. This lull in the Luftwaffe offensive had been due to weather conditions, poor visibility persisting over the South of England and the Channel. The sirens went off at around 1930 hours, when a small force of aircraft dropped around sixteen tonnes of HE and 3,600 incendiary devices before the all clear sounded just after 2215 hrs. A number of fires were started and one of them in Bedale Street had a tragic outcome. Five people were killed here that night, including four local boys and girls, Owen Spencer, Basil Travers, Doris Hadfield and Victor Allchorne. William James, an 18-year-old Auxiliary Fire Service despatch rider, also lost his life. To your right, spreading out among the railway arches, is London's oldest fruit and vegetable market, Borough Market. Already established by 1276, it is still alive and well. Try visiting here on a Friday or Saturday when the stalls are in full swing to experience the diversity of London's communities.

Bedale Street was badly bombed on 14 February 1941.

During the Great War locals would shelter from Zeppelin and Gotha bomber raids under the railway arches. Given its close proximity to London Bridge and the important railway lines overhead, it is surprising

A typical dock scene during the Blitz.

that more damage was not caused here during the Blitz. Though isolated incidents caused sporadic damage, most of the pre-war market survives today. After visiting the market continue into Cathedral Street which passes to the rear of Southwark Cathedral, visited on Walk One. From this side shrapnel damage is visible on its southern buttress.

Follow signs to the Globe, Tate and *Golden Hind* and the replica of the ship comes into view. This area of small wharfs and docks was among the first to be hit on 7 September 1940. AFS Fireman L. Bastin from Shoreditch was injured in the initial air raid and described the docks that day:

'I saw hundreds of firemen working with bombs dropping all around. I counted twelve bombs as the rescue squad carried me to a car a quarter of a mile away. On the dockside itself, right amongst the heart of those fires, civilians were standing round helping. Young girls and old men formed human chains passing buckets of water to the fireman when we could not get water from the hydrants... Throughout the worst of the bomb-dropping Police were still at work roping off streets and directing the services.

Although they could see the stupendous size of the fire, fireman going to the blaze were singing Roll out the Barrel.' (i)

Continue westbound into Clink Street and on your left are the ruins of Winchester House. This dates from 1109 and was the palace of the Bishop of Winchester. During the English Civil War it was used to house Royalist prisoners, but by the time of the Restoration it had fallen into disrepair and then lapsed into a collection of individual tenements and warehouses. A fire in one of these in 1841 revealed the remains of an impressive rose window. When, in 1941, the warehouse adjacent to it was damaged by fire once more a further archway that led through to Stoney Street was found. About this time the archaeologist Sidney Toy was able to gain access and record the find:

'The rose window was found to be in a dilapidated condition, blackened and cracked by fire and lacking many pieces. Little of this old work is now visible from the outside of the warehouses. It remains hidden from view until it shall be again revealed by a new catastrophe or by some drastic rebuilding of the area.' (ii)

Mr Toy did not have to wait long for the catastrophe. After sustaining further minor bomb damage in 1943, the existing warehouse was deemed dangerous and pulled down. At the same time, unfortunately, all traces of the Stoney Street archway were lost. The drastic rebuilding of the area

All that is left of Winchester House today.

was to follow forty years later, however, when, during a major redevelopment of Bankside, the last warehouse on this spot was demolished, revealing the rose window in its present form.

The next building on the left is the old Clink prison. By the 17th century this was one of several such establishments to be found on the South Bank.

Harsh conditions and often-flooded cells led to its eternal infamy. It still lends its name to describe any custodial sentence as 'being in the clink'. There is a small visitors' centre, tracing the history of the Clink, that makes a macabre tourist attraction. It is no surprise that, despite its underground cells, there appears to be no evidence of the local population having sheltered here during the last war. Opposite was once a large warehouse containing flour. This was destroyed in an incendiary attack early in 1941. Today its successor houses luxury waterside apartments.

Passing under the arches that carry the railway into Cannon Street Station you arrive at the junction with Bankend. Turn right towards the river. On the corner is one of London's most historic pubs, The Anchor Inn. An inn has been here for centuries. Previously known as the Castle upon the Hope, in its day it harboured escapees from the Clink in secret cubbyholes. Samuel Pepys retired here with friends during the Great Fire in 1666, describing the scene:

The Anchor at Bank End.

'*When we could endure no more we to a little alehouse in Bankside went, and stayed there until it was dark and saw the fire glow, a most horrid malicious bloody flame, it made me weep to see it. The churches, houses and all on fire and flaming at once, and a horrid noise the flames made.*' (iii)

The present building dates from the 18th century. Its upper floor and north-east corner were severely damaged by enemy action in 1941 and the repair work is clearly visible from the outside. Inside, the thirsty walker is rewarded with a pint of ale and an interesting collection of photographs from the Anchor's past, as well as a number of artefacts recovered during the redevelopment of this area.

We now pass under Southwark Bridge. This important river crossing was one of many that by November 1941 carried 6-inch steel pipes capable of carrying 5,000 gallons of water a minute. This was fed directly from the Thames by specially built pumping stations at Blackfriars and Charing

Cross.

In 1945, as part of the VE Day celebrations, Jim Morgan, by now 20 years old and a veteran with both AFS and NFS service, was taking part in a victory parade for the top brass of the Fire Service and visiting dignitaries at the Fire Brigade HQ in nearby Southwark. During their display in full parade dress and on bicycles the bells went down. Being assigned to the on-duty pump, Jim abandoned his bicycle and leapt onto the running board of the departing appliance. It was to be his first 'peacetime' fire. It was also the first time he had responded to a job without his steel helmet and as he and his vehicle flew across Southwark Bridge his best dress hat flew off and landed in the Thames, never to be seen again. Go under the arches that show the freezing-over of the Thames in 1565. This was the first of a number of years that the ice was so thick that a Frost Fair could be staged on its surface. Here you reach a stretch of the river known as Bankside. Across the Thames St Paul's comes into view and a small jetty takes visitors on pleasure trips up and down the Thames. The river is cleaner today than at any time in the last hundred years and is one of Europe's cleanest estuaries. Its brown colour comes from sediment rich in invertebrates, which in turn

Part-time firefighters. A.F.S. crew 1941.

provides a natural feeding ground for over 115 species of fish and birds. The banks of this stretch of the river were first inhabited by humans over 12,000 years ago and at low tide they still provide a good source for archaeologists.

Pass the junction with Bear Gardens, a clue to Southwark's notorious past, when alehouses, theatres and bear-baiting pits covered this area. In some ways the image of South London is still unfairly tarnished by its

Cardinal Cap Alley, beside the Globe Theatre in Southwark.

ancient history. The new model of Shakespeare's Globe Theatre is here. The original stood just off Park Street a few yards away. Its recent reconstruction has a visitors' centre, a museum, a restaurant and, of course, regular productions of the Bard's work. Then we come to a delightful row of old English houses, one of which was supposedly the residence of Sir Christopher Wren while he was overseeing the building of St Paul's. No 74, near to the narrow Cardinal Cap Alley, was severely damaged during a raid in 1941 and its entire north end above first floor level was rebuilt after the war.

The building which dominates this stretch of the South Bank is the old Bankside Power Station that now houses the Tate Modern Art Gallery, one of London's most visited attractions. The present building was converted in the late 1990s to house the Tate Modern's collection. During the war a number of power facilities stood on this spot and provided a prime target for the Luftwaffe. On 11 October 1940, unusual in that daylight sorties were carried out mainly by ME109s carrying single bombs, the evening brought heavier raids and at 1935 the power station was hit for the first time, causing damage to some of the feeders. That night over 300 Londoners were killed or wounded. Two weeks later, on 25 October, the weather cleared up sufficiently for the Luftwaffe to return in greater numbers. Raids began at 0900 and lasted until 0700 the following morning. Among the 140 people killed during this twenty-four-hour

Bankside Power Station, now the Tate Modern.

period were Walter Davis and Guy Sibley. Both worked at the transforming station in Park Road to your left.

The next time the enemy struck was on 27 June 1944, during their V1 campaign, when one of the 2,419 flying bombs to reach London hit the Southwark power station, killing Charles Reeves, a 55-year-old member of the Home Guard and Great War veteran, who was on guard at the time. As a result of the damage sustained here in the war a new power station was built in 1949. The present structure, however, dates from a Sir Giles Gilbert Scott design of 1963.

The Millennium ('wobbly') Bridge.

Here we head north, using London's latest river crossing, the Millennium Bridge. This footbridge that once famously 'wobbled', enforcing a temporary closure, is now open to the public and has become a favourite crossing for tourists and locals alike. On reaching the north side make your way up St Peter's Hill until you reach the junction with Queen Victoria Street.

The tower of St Mary Somerset.

The area to your right is almost entirely modern with the exception of the St Mary Somerset bell tower, a relic of the Wren church completed in 1695 and demolished in 1871, leaving just the tower of Portland stone that alone survived the wartime devastation in this area.

Opposite you is the College of Arms, an impressive red brick structure dating from the 1680s. Perhaps the oldest surviving building along this street, it suffered only superficial damage during the Blitz. Not so fortunate was the nearby Salvation Army Headquarters that was totally destroyed in the night of 10 May 1941. Their current HQ was opened in 1963 and is located further to the west.

Turn right in Queen Victoria Street. During the night of 29 December 1940 this street was in the middle of the serious fires surrounding St Paul's. Incendiaries were falling on this and surrounding streets at the rate of three hundred a minute. A firewatcher on duty that night describes his journey across this ground to his post on the roof of a textile warehouse:

'*Approaching the city from the south I saw by the lurid sky that the fires must be near the Cathedral and felt apprehension about our own premises. The journey on foot along Cannon Street, deserted but for fireman, was of a nightmare variety. Several big fires were in progress, particularly a large Queen Victoria Street block, the smoke and sparks of which filled the air. The sound of hostile planes overhead and the hiss of great numbers of falling incendiary bombs seemed more menacing than usual.... The roadway was a mass of fallen masonry and hosepipes interlaced towards the brow of Ludgate Hill where other fires were obtaining hold. I shall not easily forget seeing the faces of some of our firefighters in the glare, with every detail defined at a considerable distance. It would have been possible to read clearly by the light of the many fires.'* (iv)

The last major raid of the Blitz, that of 10/11 May, was to cause further damage to the landmarks along Queen Victoria Street, including No 23 whose destruction was caught on camera in one of the most dramatic photographs of the war. On this night, when over 370 German aircraft attacked the city, the civil defences were overwhelmed. Walk east as far as the security checkpoint and cross over to another Wren church, St Nicholas Cole Abbey. While not strictly an abbey (its name is believed to be a corruption of 'coldharbour' after the nearby St Paul's wharf) the original church was burnt down in 1666 and this Wren replacement was the first to be finished after the fire, opening its doors in 1677. That night in May it was completely gutted, only the charred shell remaining. In 1962 it was rebuilt under the supervision of Sir Arthur Bailey. Cutting through its small benched and paved courtyard we enter Distaff Lane. Turn left and return to St Peter's Hill. The shrapnel damage on the College of Arms building is clearly visible from here. Turn right and head up towards St Paul's Cathedral, passing Nightrider Street. At the

St Nicholas Cole Abbey.

Still visible is the blast damage to the College of Arms on Queen Victoria Street.

'Those heroes with grimy faces.'

The plaque where the Livery Hall of the Cordwainers' Company once stood.

junction with Carter Lane is the impressive memorial to London's Fire Fighters, 'those heroes with grimy faces', cast in bronze and depicting men at the end of a branch pouring water in the direction of St Paul's. Look back to the Thames. Pause here and read the names of men and women who gave their lives in the defence of London. On one November visit, while researching this book, I saw that a poppy cross had been left in memory of Bill Herbert and Harold Gillard, two AFS men of U2 Substation. Bill died of his wounds received while fighting the fire at Christ Church Broadway (visited on Walk Four) in April 1941 and Harold died on 18 September 1940 at John Lewis, Oxford Street. Both were remembered by a surviving colleague, Driver Pump Operator John Land, and so they shall be by us.

Turn left into Cannon Street and walk towards the traffic lights. Cross over and you find a sunken garden laid out like a bowling green at the junction with New Change. This was once the livery hall of the Cordwainers' Company until destroyed in 1941. A plaque commemorates the fact. This devastated area was described in 1945 by H. A. Walden:

'The results of the bombing enable us to have many new vistas of the City. Looking south from Cannon Street across devastated land through which runs Queen Victoria Street and Lower Thames Street one has glimpses of the flowing Thames. The gaunt and ruined St Nicholas Cole Abbey still

An aerial view of the devastation around St Paul's taken in 1941.

serves as an isolated landmark, buildings which had formally been obscured by adjacent blocks have a strange and unaccustomed outlook, they no longer require artificial lighting during the daytime as hitherto.' (v)

One can rest a while on a number of benches here to look at St Paul's Cathedral. This is perhaps London's most historic spot. A church was sited here as early as AD 604. Fires in 962, 1082 and 1666 destroyed later churches, so in 1939, with large-scale air attacks, the odds were stacked against Wren's cathedral.

A chapter meeting in April 1939 set out a number of measures to ensure the preservation of the Cathedral in the months ahead. These included a volunteer watch comprising staff, worshippers and citizens. One had existed during the Great War and so this was organized along similar lines. The experiences of 1914-18, however, could hardly have prepared them for what lay ahead. Mr Godfrey Allen, the Surveyor, with an intimate knowledge and love of the building, was put in charge of the watch and immediately set about recruiting, purchasing fire-fighting equipment and

St Paul's from Cannon Street in 1941.

training the various watches required to guard the cathedral by day and night. Meanwhile, inside, St Paul's was literally stripped for action in an attempt to minimize the risk to its treasures; a shelter was constructed at the west end using sandbags; the crypt was converted into a strong room where the archives were stored; hundreds of valuable books were moved to the National Library of Wales in Aberystwyth; some monuments were moved to the safety of the crypt, others too large to move such as the tomb of Nelson and the Wellington memorial were sandbagged and then bricked in place in an attempt to minimize blast. Wellington's tomb, constructed of masses of Cornish porphyry and granite, was considered indestructible and left unprotected. A first aid unit was set up in the cathedral to deal with potential casualties to staff and manned by personnel from the Red Cross and St John Ambulance services. A control room was established which was connected to the various fire-watching stations situated around the cathedral and in the dome itself. Emergency water supplies were fitted by the London Fire Brigade. The west end of the building was made gas-proof. Food stores were laid in, together with cooking appliances. St Paul's was in effect gearing up for a siege.

By early September the bells fell silent and London, its breath held, waited. As we know, a year of inactivity followed and this enabled the watches to hone their wartime duties. The first bombs to drop near St Paul's were on 25 August 1940 when a small force of German aircraft reached London. Two bombs were dropped but caused no damage. The real Blitz started two weeks later in the early evening of 7 September. The docks were the main targets that night and a watch member recalls:

'Some of us watched the bombardment from the colonnade of St Paul's. It was a golden, peaceful evening and, as the light faded from the sky, the angry red glow in the east, diversified by leaping flames, dominated the prospect, while from time to time the peculiar thud of bursting bombs punctured the silence... at last someone spoke, "It is like the end of the world," and someone else replied, "It is the end of the world".' (vi)

We now walk round the cathedral to look at a number of incidents that were to occur in the following months. New Change, one of the oldest streets in London, continues north and just at the foot of St Paul's can be

From the dome of St Paul's looking back up Cannon Street in 1944.

found another church tower, St Augustine's with St Faith's, one of the ring of Wren churches that surrounded St Paul's. Destroyed during the winter of 1940, its tower was saved and was incorporated into the post-war choir school. The tulip dome and black lead spire are a result of this reconstruction. The wartime choirschool boys were evacuated in August 1939 to Truro in Cornwall where they continued to sing in the Cathedral until it was safe for them to return to London.

The road layout surrounding St Paul's has changed greatly since the war. We enter St Paul's Churchyard via the iron gates. This was once an important thoroughfare but is now a secluded garden. Be warned that these are locked after dark. Walk past the east end of the Cathedral and, after a short while the gardens open up and you see the site of St Paul's Cross. Here on the night of 16 April 1941 a dramatic incident took place. Mr Gerald Henderson, a member of the watch, describes the events:

'*Shortly after 4am I discovered a sea mine enveloped in a green silk parachute at the north-east corner of the cathedral. It was about eight foot high and lay close to the site of St Paul's Cross. I was somewhat dazed by the events of the night and did not realize at once what the shrouded object may be. It crossed my mind that the silk may have been blown out of some warehouse. I went up to the place and drew aside the silk covering. It then appeared that the object beneath it was a shining steel sea mine. It was like an elongated pear in shape and had rows of horns at the top and bottom... .I was afraid that I might cause the mine to topple over if I dragged the covering silk and remained still and perplexed for some little time, holding the silk in my hands.*' (vii)

Eventually Gerald reported the incident to the Police Station in Snow Hill. After some delay the police officer in charge reported the matter to the Admiralty and a constable was despatched to make a report:

'*When we arrived at the Cheapside gate to the Churchyard I unlocked it and was putting my keys back into my pocket when the constable, somewhat agitated, said, "I should leave the keys and your helmet here if I were you sir. These things go off, they say, if any steel is brought near them." I took him towards the cathedral and, having peered at the object through the shrubs, he said he had seen enough and departed!*'

St Paul's Cross where the parachute mine fell.

In time the naval team arrived and proceeded to deal

with the mine. It was then removed (with its silk parachute to the disappointment of its discoverer) but not before some further drama. While the device was being made safe, a fire engine, against Police instructions, was driven at full speed past the scene towards Cannon Street. This caused the mechanism to start up, but the ticking stopped when the last horn was removed.

A little further on can be found a modern memorial set into the ground, commemorating the people of London in wartime. It was erected in conjunction with the *Evening Standard* and makes use of the Edward Marsh quotation often attributed to Churchill:

> *In war resolution, In defeat defiance, In victory magnanimity, In peace goodwill.*

Leaving by the wrought iron gates you emerge at the entrance to the crypt which now houses a café. Entrance to the Cathedral itself costs £6.00. Like Westminster Abbey, it requires a few hours to look around. Justice to its long history is not the aim of this book, so from the outside we will dwell on more of the building's wartime escapades. Walk to the south-west corner of the cathedral and some granite pillars can be seen. Between these and the road surface a 1000kg bomb fell and penetrated the surface at an angle, finally coming to rest underneath the clock tower, fifteen feet down. On examination, it was discovered to not be a dud but armed with a long-delay fuse, protected by an anti-tamper device. The area was sealed off, but work could not start for a whole day due to a nearby severed gas main. The size and location of the bomb meant that if it were to explode the cathedral would suffer severe if not disastrous structural damage, so the bomb disposal team, led by Lieutenant Robert Davies, decided to remove the device intact. When the excavations began the men

This shows the hits in and around St Paul's Cathedral.

cautiously dug around the device and it lurched another twelve feet below the surface. The operation had to start all over again, with the threat of any sudden movement setting off the mechanism and the slippery clay around

It was here that Lieutenant Davies and his team saved St Paul's.

the bomb making it almost impossible to get any purchase to remove it. The work was slow. At last, on the morning of 15 September, the mud-caked, evil-looking bomb was lifted, using steel hawsers and pulleys before being carefully placed on the rear of a pair of trucks pulled up in tandem. A car bearing a red flag led the lorries and their dangerous cargo at high speed through the streets of London before reaching Hackney Marshes where it could be disposed of safely. The driver of the truck was Lieutenant Robert Davies himself, who had not wished to put his men to any further risk. For this and for his efforts over the whole four days he and Sapper George Wylie, a member of his team, were awarded the George Cross. Further awards of the BEM followed for both Sergeant Jim Wilson and Lance Corporal Bert Leigh.

Some parts of St Paul's were damaged during the next year. The first direct hit occurred on 10 October 1940 when at 5.55am a high-explosive bomb penetrated the roof of the choir and detonated west of the apse, bringing down the roof of the transverse arch and ripping a hole in the vault. Tons of masonry came crashing down from a height of 90 feet, but, amazingly, did not cause the crypt roof to collapse. The Archdeacon of London had been sleeping just below. Another verger, Mr R. Leese, described the incident:

' *I had just gone out onto the east roof of the choir when I heard the loud swishing noise which meant that bombs were coming down very close. I judged that there were three of four. Automatically I threw myself down full length in the gutter of the roof. There was a loud bang and I felt as if my whole body was being compressed. When I looked up there was a black cloud of dust and smoke and dust over the roof and through it I could see a large whole as if a giant had taken a bite out of it.'* (viii)

On 16/17 April 1941, during the same raid that the parachute mine was discovered by St Paul's Cross, a HE bomb struck the north transept at 2.50am. Those inside the cathedral at the time described it as being like an earthquake. Those in the crypt, on the roof or the floor of the church felt the entire building shake. The west and east doors were destroyed, the

A sketch of the cathedral in 1941.

remaining windows were blown out, iron framework was twisted and buckled, the Corinthian columns destroyed. The east and west transept walls bulged outwards but the dome somehow remained intact. St Paul's had survived again. The final damage to the cathedral was during the heavy raid of 10/11 May when the rest of London was also suffering the worst night of the Blitz. The by now experienced St Paul's staff dealt with four incendiary bombs on the roof, but a number of HE bombs landing close by left the building chipped, dishevelled and pockmarked, damage that remains visible today. Before we leave St Paul's the final word must go to a roof spotter atop a nearby textile factory:

'It was an awe-inspiring and wonderful sight for those of us who witnessed it.

'St Paul's cathedral, ringed by raging fires and falling masonry, its great dome superimposed and reddened all night by reflected flames, seemed to take upon itself an even greater dignity, as it stood in the midst of the example of man's inhumanity to man.' (ix)

We head down Ludgate Hill turning right into Ave Maria Lane. The area to your right is Paternoster Square. At the time of writing this is again under major reconstruction. Prior to the war this area had been home to numerous publishers and textile companies, but most of it was destroyed in the firebomb attack of 29 December 1940. Some, like Hitchcock Williams and Sons, had organized an efficient system of roof spotters and fire staff. Unfortunately, given the close proximity of neighbouring premises with inadequate arrangements, even their best efforts could not save their own buildings. At the height of the raid Hitchcocks had over 100 staff fighting the numerous blazes in the vicinity. The adjacent St Paul's Chapter House, built by Wren, was alight and the company's old building at 69/70 St Paul's Churchyard had also caught fire. Three times the police advised the firewatchers to evacuate the building as it was a lost cause. Eventually they were dragged out of the burning building by the manager, utterly exhausted. Among the millions of pounds worth of damage caused to the company that night they also lost the prize money for their New Year Draw, the framed Roll of Honour for staff members in the 1914-18 war and the room where Sir George Williams had formed the YMCA in 1844. One

The blitzed premises of Hitchcock Williams.

Paternoster Square after the demolition squads had finished.

staff member was distraught at the loss of an Iron Cross given to him in France in 1916 by a German prisoner of war. He had left it in his desk drawer after showing it to his colleagues.

By February 1941, after continual raids, the area was totally devastated:

> *'The scene of desolation in the area at the rear of our building was terrible. It could be likened to the result of an earthquake. Publishers, publicans, booksellers, scent makers, cafes, solicitors, in fact all branches of the professions and industry suffered. Notices and papers strung along railings and ropes indicating location of new or temporary addresses could be compared with washing hanging on a line.'* (x)

Soon the demolition squads moved in and levelled the area flat between St Paul's and Newgate Street. Some of the rubble found its way to America. The rest, in an ultimate act of defiance, ended up forming the concrete piers used in the D-Day landings! What was left became a large public car park. Some cellars were flooded to provide emergency water supplies for civil defence and a number of large round canvas water dams were erected to supplement these. Impromptu rockeries grew up, covered with ragwort, scabious, poppies and rosebay willow herb. In less than a year nature was reclaiming the city. An NFS unit cleared and cultivated a vegetable garden and bred pigs, poultry and rabbits in the basements of ruined buildings. The burnt-out framework of Messrs Grossmiths building was used by the local Home Guard for training in street fighting and grenade throwing.

We are now in Warwick Lane and on the left are the only pre-war buildings to be found here, notably the Cutler's Hall. On reaching Newgate Street cross over, stop and look west. The Scales of Justice are visible on top of the Central Criminal Court, more commonly known as the Old Bailey. This was built in 1903 on the foundations of Newgate Prison. Its stonework can be seen at the foot of the present building. The Old Bailey was severely damaged when its north-west wing was torn away and Court No 2 was destroyed.

The Cutlers' Hall today.

We walk east from here and a small garden opens up on the right. This is Greyfriars Passage, originally a burial site for the nearby Christ Church.

The plaque at the entrance to Greyfriars Passage.

From 1841, however, this has been designated an open space. An old parish notice board on the railings tells us that the church was destroyed by enemy action. The building ahead of us, today a dental practice, has a plaque on its wall stating that it was once the vestry for Christ Church before being partly burnt out in 1940.

Take the narrow walkway between Greyfriars Passage and the dentists and you arrive at the entrance to the shell of Christ Church, Newgate Street. The church is another example of Wren's work. It was completely destroyed in the raids of 1940 and 1941 and today is an open garden for quiet rest and reflection. For us it marks the end of our walk and, indeed, the book and our journey together. Set among the fire-blackened shell of the church, with its benches and rose garden, there is, perhaps, no more suitable memorial to the victims of the Blitz and marks the perfect place for us to look back on all we have seen on our walks. In the shadow of the dome of St Paul's we can see that, while London is today a modern forward-thinking city, its past is never far from view and, despite its suffering during the war years, the severe loss of life and damage and destruction to many of its most historic and famous buildings, our capital ultimately proved the old wartime phrase, LONDON CAN TAKE IT!

St Paul's underground station is situated just a short walk away, lest we forget.

(i) - *I Was There* – John Hammerton – Amalgamated Press 1941

(ii) - *A Blueprint for London* – Sidney Toy 1946

(iii) - *A Londoner's Diary* – Samuel Pepys

(iv) - *Operation Textiles* – H A Walden – Thos Reed & Co 1945

(v) - As above

(vi) - *St Paul's Cathedral in Wartime* – W R Mathews – Hutchinsons 1946

(vii) - As above

(viii) - As above

(ix) - *Operation Textiles* – H A Walden – Thos Reed & Co 1945

(x) - As above

The steeple, all that remains of Christ Church, Newgate Street.

London before the war. An aerial photograph taken in 1935.

APPENDIX I

BRITAIN'S CIVIL DEFENCE – Equipment & Tactics

This appendix is intended to give the reader a basic understanding of the various branches engaged in the home defence of the United Kingdom during the war.

In 1939 memories of the Great War were still very much at the forefront of the public's and the authorities' thinking. One lesson in particular had been learnt: that the development of air power would play a major role in any conflict. The civilian population would be subjected to an intense, sustained bombing campaign designed to destroy the infrastructure and manufacturing capability of the nation – as well as the morale of its people. Also very evident was the fact that London would be the primary target of any such strike.

In the build-up to the Second World War a number of leading politicians and commentators published works on the expected size of the Luftwaffe forces and the anticipated effect they would have on Britain. Whilst these figures tended to vary erratically, most drew evidence from statistics gathered during the Zeppelin and Gotha bomber raids of the Great War. During this period less than 75 tons of bombs had been dropped on Britain and just over 2,900 people had been killed or wounded.

When in 1938 the then Lord Chancellor predicted that the Germans would be in a position to drop 3,000 tons of bombs a day it must be remembered that he was delivering a speech attempting to justify the recent Munich Agreement. At the other end of the scale, Basil Liddell Hart, author of *The Defence of Britain*, made the more conservative estimate of 600 tons of ordnance a day over a drawn-out bombing campaign. Working from a number of these estimates the Ministry of Health issued a warning that it could be expected that 1,800,000 citizens would be killed or wounded in the opening six months of the war.

Intended to prevent this catastrophe were a number of military and civil defence mechanisms, each with an individual part to play but combining to create the basis of the country's home defence.

The Chain Home System

Hastily erected just prior to the war along a line that stretched from Portsmouth in the south to Aberdeen in the north were twenty Radio Direction Finding (RDF) stations. Later after the entry of the Americans into the war, these would be more commonly known as RADAR. In 1940 they were able to detect the location, altitude (provided it was above 15,000 feet) and approximate strength of the raiders roughly 100 miles off the coast of Britain. An early experimental success was the tracking of Chamberlain's aircraft on its way to Munich for his meeting with Adolf Hitler in September 1938. Each station consisted of a varying number of 360-foot steel transmitting towers and 240-foot wooden receiving towers connected to a small operations room. This room was manned by a sergeant and his team of RAF and WAAF operators. Working round the clock, they would convert the information obtained and forward it to Fighter Command at Bentley Priory. As anticipated, a number of these stations were heavily raided by enemy aircraft and some damaged during the Battle of Britain, but the overlapping coverage of the sites enabled the system to remain operational throughout.

RAF Fighter Command

Located near Stanmore in Middlesex, it was from this vital command centre that Air Chief Marshal Sir Hugh Dowding directed his mixed force of, in the main, Hurricanes and Spitfires, which amounted to approximately forty operational squadrons designated for the defence of Great Britain. The Filter Centre at Bentley would receive plots of aircraft approaching the coast from the RDFs and, until proved otherwise, these would be marked as 'hostile' on their large plotting tables. From here information would be passed to a centralized operations room situated in the same complex and then passed on to group and sector operations that between them would scramble the most appropriate resources to engage the approaching enemy. Once aircraft were airborne the sector controllers directed the engagement, ensuring the fighters had the latest information of altitude, direction and strengths. On contact with the enemy by sight the leader of the respective fighter force would take control from ground operations with the call of 'Tally-Ho', at which stage the sector controller could monitor the action via the radio traffic passed between aircraft. On completion of the engagement the sector controller would once again take control until the aircraft returned to base.

The Royal Observer Corps

At five-mile intervals around the southern and eastern coast were the 1,400 small and often isolated posts of the Royal Observer Corps. Able to spot the lower-flying aircraft that RDFs had not seen, these cramped sandbagged emplacements, (situated on hilltops to provide unbroken views) were manned by two observers armed with binoculars, a height finder and a landline back to Observer Group headquarters. These mostly part-time men and women were able to provide the location, direction, strength and type of aircraft for their headquarters who in turn liaised with Fighter Command's sector operations rooms. Their most important piece of equipment, however, was their sharp eyesight and acute hearing that enabled them quickly and efficiently to locate the enemy, regardless of weather or daylight.

Anti-Aircraft Defences

Again communications played a key role in this area of air defence. Anti-aircraft batteries could only be used when the sky was clear of friendly aircraft, so constant liaison with fighter command was vital. The job of running an efficient anti-aircraft command fell to General Sir Frederick Pile, appointed only a few weeks before the war started. Two types of anti-aircraft gun were employed by A.A. Command in great numbers, these being the 3.7 inch which was capable of firing ten 28-pound shells per minute, which exploded via a timing fuse scattering fragments that could damage aircraft within a 15-yard radius. This gun was useful to a ceiling of 25,000 feet. Secondly, the 4.5 inch which fired 55-pound shells at a maximum rate of eight a minute up to 26,000 feet, effective within 20 yards of detonation. Used in far smaller numbers were the 3 inch guns of Great War vintage mounted on an updated carriage that had a limited ceiling of 14,000 feet. The highly effective and reliable Bofors gun provided cover against low-flying raiders. Their rapid rate of fire (120 rounds a minute) and 2-pound high explosive shells had a ceiling of 12,000

St Paul's in wartime, protected by a solitary LZ balloon.

feet, above which they self-detonated to render themselves harmless as they fell to the ground. It must be remembered that the dual role of an anti-aircraft barrage is not only to shoot down enemy aircraft but also to try and force them away from their intended target area.

During night raids sound locators would pick up hostile aircraft formations nearing their target, searchlight batteries would attempt to illuminate the enemy raiders by means of a 90cm light that provided a 210 million candlewatt beam. These were capable of dazzling enemy pilots and rendering them incapable of accurately locating their intended target.

Over the target area flew the final part of our air defence, the barrage balloons. The 65-foot-long LZ (low zone) balloon was moored to a mobile winch that was capable of launching it from its resting height of 500 feet to its ceiling height of 5,000 feet in around ten minutes. Between four and five hundred balloons were required for an effective barrage over London. This provided a one in ten chance of bringing down a low-flying raider with the aid of its 'double parachute link' system. When an aircraft struck a balloon cable two cutting links were activated that released the centre section of cable. Two parachutes were then automatically opened and the weight/drag was sufficient to bring down the hostile aircraft. Throughout the war around a hundred aircraft were brought down (a number of them friendly), but the true value of the balloons was that they pushed the enemy aircraft higher and thus reduced the effectiveness of their bombing.

The balloons were vulnerable to poor weather conditions, however, and on one infamous night in September 1939 an electrical storm brought down and destroyed seventy-eight of them. Overall the sound of anti-aircraft batteries in action and the sight of balloons overhead did much to calm the nerves of many a Londoner during the Blitz. At a time when its overseas forces were experiencing little success, the constant crump-crump of these batteries in some small way were a means of hitting back at Hitler.

Air Raid Precaution Wardens

Though today immortalized by Warden Hodges shouting 'Put that light out,' the ARP warden was in the main a committed, quick-thinking, level-headed member of the community who was to prove vital during the Blitz. Often they worked flat out with little sleep, and then got up to continue with their day jobs.

In 1935 the Home Office had set up an ARP department tasked with planning for the mass evacuation of cities, the training of gas and bomb precautions and the wholesale expansion of fire services that would be required if Britain was subjected to a large-scale bombing campaign. The

A suburban A.R. P. wardens' post share a private joke with their camera-shy cat.

ARP Act of 1937 passed responsibility from Whitehall to local authorities who estimated that around 400,000 wardens would be required nationwide. Split into a dozen regions, No 5 covered Greater London, controlling its own area with reporting centres, control rooms and subdivided into sectors. An individual warden post was staffed by six wardens who would cover around 500 people; about one in six wardens were women. The phoney war period was a bad time for ARP wardens, many of the population regarding them as Nosey Parkers or 'draft dodgers'. Soon after Dunkirk, however, this was to change as the threat of invasion was suddenly very realistic and, when the bombing did arrive, the 'Cinderella Service' was finally to prove itself to the community.

The dual roles of the warden were to act as the eyes and ears of the Civil Defence control rooms by reporting in a manner which neither under- nor over- estimated the severity of the situation. Secondly, by giving out clear, concise instructions to members of the public during a raid, they were able to gain their trust and confidence, leading them to the shelter at night, pulling them free from debris if the rescue services had yet to arrive and making their nightly rounds to the shelters. Overall the warden had to act as a 'good neighbour' during the Blitz.

London's Police Services

The City of London, Metropolitan, Auxiliary Police War Reserve and Special Constabulary forces not only went about the daily business of keeping Londoners safe (the blackout period led to a dramatic increase in certain offences and road traffic accidents), they also took on the task of every other Civil Defence service, dealing with incendiary bombs so as not to trouble the Fire Brigade, rescuing trapped people and assisting the wounded, evacuating areas, diverting traffic, preventing looting by securing or guarding insecure premises such as blown-in shop windows. It also fell to the police after an incident to count the casualties, advise the next of kin and deal with the streams of incoming enquiries following a raid. Despite the unique administrative arrangement in London whereby the Metropolitan Police reported to the Home Office and not the local authorities, many a constable worked shoulder to shoulder with the Civil Defence, so that even in wartime they were able to uphold the worthy traditions of the British Police Force.

'Your Special Constabulary needs you.'

A mixed group of regular, special and wartime policemen.

A police watch in wartime.

London's Fire Services

Pre-war London's professional firefighters were employed by the local authority and manned fifty-nine regular fire stations and three river stations around the city. At that time the London Fire Brigade was still largely made up from men of both the Royal and Merchant Navy and was a highly motivated and well-trained force. While this proved adequate in peacetime the 1937 Civil Defence Act estimated that an additional 28,000 men would be required in London during wartime and the Auxiliary Fire Service was born. Less that two years later 23,000 volunteers had been raised, trained and equipped and were manning over 300 additional stations to assist their regular counterparts. In the beginning the AFS were regarded with suspicion by the LFB men who thought that their jobs may be at risk and accused them of being 'three quid a week army dodgers'. When the Blitz did start on 7 September 1940 it has been estimated that almost four-fifths of the AFS had not yet seen a fire, yet they were about to fight the largest conflagrations seen in the city since 1666. By this time a growing number of AFS men had began to integrate with the regular forces, due to sickness or shortages. These men, known as 'red-riders' on account of them manning the traditional red fire appliances owned by the LFB as opposed to the grey engines of the AFS, gained valuable experience and broke down a number of barriers between the regular and part-time organizations.

The main appliance used by the LFB was the heavy pump, carrying a huge steel turntable and mobile fire-escape ladders, and capable of

Regular London firefighters prewar.

throwing a jet of 900 gallons of water a minute up to 100 feet in the air. These vehicles were assisted by hose-laying lorries that could lay up to 6,000 feet of rubberized hosing at a speed of twenty miles an hour drawing vitally needed water from the River Thames or the numerous EWS (emergency water supplies), often canvas dams or flooded basements of blitzed buildings situated around the city. The AFS were primarily equipped with trailer pumps issued by the Home Office. These light appliances were easily handled by two or three men and were able to pump 500 gallons of water a minute. They were towed behind commandeered London taxis painted grey, which also carried the men, hoses and additional fire-fighting equipment. There were over a thousand such pumps situated in central London and many thousands more were available if required in the suburbs.

On 18 August 1941 it was decided that all the various fire brigades around the county, both regular and auxiliary, should be amalgamated and the National Fire Service was created. In the preceding twelve months gleaming red engines had been painted khaki, polished headgear replaced with steel helmets, shining brass covered with camouflaged paint, gas masks had been issued and thousands of new battleship grey engines of the AFS were standing by at commandeered buildings now temporary fire stations,

London's fire services were now not only fighting fires they were fighting a war.

The Rescue Service

Another important branch in the Civil Defence forces were the rescue squads. These volunteers would arrive at the scene of an occurrence, often before the area had been cleared of unexploded bombs, and work their way through the rubble. They developed the art of tunnelling in a zigzag fashion, shoring the roof up with makeshift bits of furniture in the knowledge that they could get out with the rescued by the same way as they had come in. Every few minutes the squad leader would call for quiet and all hands would then listen for the telltale signs of life. Fires, floods, gas and the collapse of buildings were all hazards of work for these men, who, distinguishable by their steel helmets marked 'R' and their shelter suits, stuck to the task throughout the night regardless of any off-duty time,

> 'We done all the rough work, see, twelve hours it might 'a bin, and then they want to send us home and let these reinforcement chaps from Walthamstow get the old boy out! – Not if I could help it!' Anon, rescue man *Home Front HMSO 1942*

A First Aid party dressed for war.

First Aid Services

These small teams of four or five first-aid-trained men provided the initial medical assistance at incidents normally while the raid was still in progress; by early 1941 they were also assisted by an incident doctor. They prioritized casualties and provided basic first aid before the injured were evacuated to hospitals. This was by a fleet of ambulances, the drivers of which were often female and recruited from the upper classes of London, having learnt to drive pre-war. No instructor, though, could have prepared them for the war-torn, often impassable streets they were to negotiate during the Blitz.

Women's Voluntary Service

The provision of food, shelter and clothing was undertaken by the WVS, created in 1938 to work alongside the ARP. Mobile canteens were sent to both incident scenes and rest shelters, from which sandwiches, hot tea and a wad were available to rescuers and the rescued alike, just as they were to my colleagues and myself working at the Hatfield rail crash in 2000. Blankets and clothing were issued to air-raid victims at rest shelters and

A mixed group of Civil Defence Volunteers.

field kitchens serving hot food were established in bombed areas via the King's Messenger convoys.

The YMCA, the British Red Cross, St John Ambulance, the GPO, Gas, Water and Electricity boards also played their part in a huge humanitarian effort, together with the average Londoner, who, despite living under the constant threat of losing their own lives or property, stood shoulder to shoulder and declared to the world 'London can take it!'

APPENDIX II

THE LUFTWAFFE – Organization & Equipment

On the declaration of war in September 1939 it is estimated from German records that around 1,200 aircraft were capable of engaging the United Kingdom in a bombing campaign from their home soil. This figure was considerably lower than the British Government had reckoned on in their 'worst case scenario figures' earlier that year. The vast majority of the aircraft available to the Luftwaffe were twin-engine Heinkel 111s backed

The first raid, 9 September 1940. German aircraft over Abbey Wood and Thamesmead, South London.

up by around 400 Dornier 17s, both of which suffered from the fact that for them to reach Britain extra fuel was required which drastically cut down on their bomb loads. When fully loaded with fuel and ordnance they were restricted to a maximum speed of 190mph, which left them vulnerable to almost all of the Royal Air Forces fighters deployed on home defence. When considering that the distance also meant that no fighter cover was possible for German bomber crews it becomes clear that it was not until the fall of France that Britain and London became a realistic target.

After Dunkirk this was the case and the German High Command sought to use the Luftwaffe to destroy the already depleted Royal Air Force and break British morale in preparation for their planned invasion. Two formations were chosen to spearhead the bombing campaign:

Luftflotte 2, commanded by *Generalfeldmarschall* Albert Kesselring from his headquarters in Brussels and made up from units stationed east of the River Seine operating from Holland, Belgium and Northern France.

Luftflotte 3, commanded by *Generalfeldmarschall* Hugo Sperrle from his headquarters in Paris and made up from units stationed west of the River Seine operating from Northern France.

These were backed up by a smaller force Luftflotte 5, operating from Denmark and Norway and commanded by *Generalfeldmarschall* Hans-Juergen Stumpff from his Olso headquarters. In total this provided a maximum operational strength of just fewer than 1,600 long-range bombers backed up by 1,200 fighters.

While many types and variants of aircraft were employed against London during the Blitz the following aircraft formed the majority:

Heinkel 111 – In operational service with the Luftwaffe from 1936, this medium-range bomber with a crew of five had a ceiling of 6,500 metres and a top speed of 252mph. It provided the bulk of aircraft used in raids on London during the opening weeks of the Blitz; armaments included three 7.92mm machine guns and the ability to carry a 2,000kg bomb load.

Junkers 88 – Arguably the Luftwaffe's most efficient medium-range bomber in service during the Blitz; its ceiling at 8,200 metres and top speed of 292mph outperformed the HE111 and its crew of four were able to operate up to seven machine guns. However, its bomb load was lower, with a capability of 500kgs internally stored and 1,000kgs externally.

Dornier 17 – Nicknamed the flying pencil due to its long thin profile, this aircraft came into service in early 1939. With a ceiling of 8,200 metres it was the quickest of the three main bombers employed, with a top speed of 348mph. Its four-man crew were armed with seven machine guns, but a smaller bomb load capacity of just 1,000kgs.

Messerschmitt 110 – this long-range multi-seat escort fighter had a

Cleaning up after a heavy raid in London.

range of 482 miles, its two-man crew were armed with two cannons and four machine guns in the nose, plus a rear-facing machine gun. Its top speed of 349mph led to disastrous results when it came into contact with RAF Spitfires and Hurricanes during the Battle of Britain, leading to it requiring an escort fighter itself. With the ability to carry an external bomb load of 1,000kgs, it was later successfully employed as a night fighter.

Messerschmitt 109 – This excellent fighter escort was well armed with a good turn of speed at 387mph. Its range shortage was in part overcome by plywood fuel drop tanks that enabled it to operate for a short period over London. If required, it too could carry up to 250kgs of bombs externally.

The were many different bombs dropped on London during the Blitz. These fit into six main groups as follows:

SC class – used for demolition purposes, this high explosive bomb with a very strong blast effect consisting of 55% explosive and provided the workhorse of the Luftwaffe. They made up almost 80% of all HE bombs dropped on the capital and came in numerous sizes from the commonly used SC50 (weighing 50 kgs), SC250, SC500, SC1000, SC1200, SC1800, SC2000, through to the largest SC2500, the heaviest bomb to be dropped on London during the Blitz. Made in three sections with a thick nose welded onto thin steel walls and an alloy tail, they sometimes had a ring fitted known as a *kopfring* around the nose to prevent them from penetrating too far below ground and ensuring maximum blast above the surface. Smaller versions were occasionally adapted to carry cardboard windpipes so as to whistle when falling. This had both an adverse effect on morale and could also mask the sound of falling bombs set with delayed-action fuses that would lie undetected until such time as their fuses primed them.

SD class – anti-personnel or partially armour-piercing, they carried a smaller 35% explosive, but had a more efficient fragmentation effect as they were constructed from a single piece of steel. Again coming in a variety of sizes, their names also indicate their weight in kilograms: SD50, SD70, SD250, SD500 and the SD1700. *Kopfrings* were not uncommon in the larger-sized bombs.

PC class – armour-piercing and designed to be used against heavy fortifications or shipping, they contained 20% explosive and were constructed of a heavy steel nose and walls. Used in London to a far lesser extent than the SC class, they came in three sizes: PC500, PC1000 and the largest, PC1400, converted to a radio-controlled bomb by the end of the war.

Luftmine class – These aerial mines were initially designed for use against shipping and were, therefore, magnetic. They were dropped by

A wartime policeman keeping the public away from an unexploded bomb.

parachute initially in British coastal waters. This led to the Admiralty gaining an expertise in dealing with them that ensured an unlikely Royal Naval presence in London during the Blitz. For use against urban targets a clockwork fuse was fitted ensuring detonation. This would normally activate after twenty-five seconds. The LMA weighed 500kgs, whilst the larger LMB weighed 1000kgs. The BM1000 was a later design that worked off of a photoelectric cell device that would detonate on exposure to the light following the breaking away of its Bakelite tail. It should be noted that the destructive capability of between 60 and 70% explosives of these landmines were similar to that of a V1 Flying Bomb.

Easily the most destructive bomb employed by the Luftwaffe during the Blitz was the Incendiary Bomb used in various shapes and sizes from the common 1kg and 2kg IBs dropped in such numbers on the fire raid of 29 December 1940 to the heavier 250kg or 500kg oil bombs that destroyed parts of buildings such as St Margaret's Church in Westminster.

The smaller IBs contained magnesium that burnt at temperatures that could melt steel and were designed to penetrate roof tiles but lodge in hard-to-reach lofts and rafters. When released in great numbers from containers that blew open at a predetermined height, these spread themselves over a wide area. The risk to Civil Defence personnel working on the ground being struck by these was also severe.

Finally we should mention the Butterfly Bomb. The most commonly used anti-personnel device used over Britain, the SD2, as it was officially known, weighed 2kg and was dropped in batches of twenty or more in a container that again blew open at a predetermined height. Once released, the outer shell opened up revealing a set of wings which, as it spun down to earth, would ingeniously wind up or prime the mechanical fuse arming the device. It was set off by anyone touching the device and as such the only means of disposal was by controlled explosion from a safe distance.

The V1 Flying Bomb (Doodlebug)

On 13 June 1944 a new strange sound was heard in the skies above London, initially the buzzing, flame-spluttering, dark, flying objects were mistaken for 'downed raiders' by anti-aircraft gunners and civilians alike. Over the next five days 500 unmanned flying bombs had been launched from their bases in northern France by the 155 (W) Flak Regiment. Hitler's vengeance campaign had begun.

In essence the V1 was a pilotless monoplane, 25ft long with a wingspan of 17ft. After being catapulted from its purpose-built launch ramp, it sped at an average of 350mph at an optimum height of between 3-4000 feet for a range of approximately 130 miles before reaching its target. Direction

The aftermath of a flying bomb. Sergeant Robinson and his colleagues show the signs of shock and exhaustion which followed such incidents.

was maintained by the aid of a gyroscopic unit that stabilized the rudder and elevators via a pre set compass. After a set distance the elevators would be automatically depressed and the missile would dive towards its target. Just behind the nose was a warhead that contained 850kg of high explosive designed to explode on impact with the minimum penetration and maximum blast effect.

By the last week in June these terror weapons were heading towards London at a rate of over 100 a day. My grandfather was at that time based at Tilbury in the lead-up to D-Day. He remembers the distinctive sound of the doodlebugs flying along the Thames estuary day and night *en route* to the capital. They acted as the biggest motivator for all who saw them prior to the Normandy landings. Their destructive capability is well recorded and in total nearly 2,500 reached London before their launch sites were finally overrun in March 1945. The cost in human terms was 24,000 casualties of which over 6,000 were killed countrywide (over 9,000 V1s were launched at the United Kingdom in total). The following account is by Mike Borrow OBE who grew up in London during wartime,

'On Wednesday 12 July 1944 I was coming back from Southampton by train and we were approaching Waterloo station just by Battersea between 3 and 4 in the afternoon. Standing in the corridor, leaning on the window rail looking west over London a flying bomb appeared running parallel to us in the same direction. As we were on the viaduct it came abreast of us diving to the right and into a building, raising a column of debris and smoke. Although there were several of us in the corridor, American serviceman and civilians, I cannot remember anyone ducking from the anticipated blast or making a remark, perhaps because we were observers only, and did not hear, and we were not expecting the cut out and most of all the deafening silence before it hit.'

The V2 Rocket

Hitler's last secret weapon was to be used against London for the first time on the night of 8 September 1944. Like a bolt of lightning a V2 fell on Chiswick killing three people and seriously wounding another seventeen people. Between then and 29 May 1945 1,145 such rockets would be launched against this country. The V2 was a 46ft-high rocket stabilized by four large fins. Its nose contained a warhead capable of delivering a ton of explosive. Fully loaded, it also carried 9 tons of alcohol and liquid oxygen fuel. It was fired vertically from a small concrete hard-standing or an improvised log platform. This meant that its launch site was highly mobile, the rockets being transported on custom-made trailer trucks. Once fired, the V2 flew at a height of 50-60 miles maintaining a speed of 3,500

Savile Row Police Station showing the scars of war.

mph. Its range was accurate up to 225 miles. Of the 517 V2s fired at London perhaps the most tragic incident occurred in New Cross Road, Deptford, when Woolworths was hit on 25 November 1944. The death toll was officially 160 but is widely reported as being much higher. At least a further 100 people were seriously wounded. Despite the introduction of this new terror weapon, the spirit of the Londoners did still not crack, though the final casualty figures were as high as 9,277, nearly 3,000 of whom were killed countrywide (note: this was considerably lower than those for the V1). The following account by Robert Henrey shows the fascination with the rockets as late as December 1944,

'The news that the Thames had swallowed up a V2 was sufficiently known by the Monday morning for people to peer over the Embankment to discover exactly where it dropped...leaning against the Embankment parapet, an old man with a pitted red face was pointing with a short clay pipe, the bowl turned downwards, in the direction of the mudflats on the opposite shore, see where them pebbles are, thrown up by the explosion they was the mud's littered with em.' (ii)

(i) – *Private memoirs of Mike Borrow OBE*
(ii) – *The Siege of London* – Robert Henrey – Temple Press 1946

Associated Visits

London is a city of many museums and places of interest. However, due to their locations, two essential visits for anyone interested in London in wartime have been omitted from the walks in this book. If possible, time should be set aside to visit the following to make their Blitz experience complete,

The Imperial War Museum, Lambeth Road, SE1

Now with free admission, this extensive museum is open between 10.00 – 18.00 daily and has a number of permanent Blitz-related exhibits. Firstly, the hall that deals with the Second World War contains many home-front items, including artefacts, equipment, films and audio clips presented in a user-friendly manner. There is even computer access to the Civilian Roll of Honour. In a separate room the 1940s house is an excellent way to view how we used to live. As you walk around, evocative period music drifts through the air and it must be confessed that it was a visit here in the spring of 2001 inspired me to sit down and write this book. Not to be missed is the Blitz Experience where you are instructed by museum staff, (the best ones act as if ARP wardens) to enter a shelter where, after a short but violent bombardment and a near miss, you leave and are led through a diorama of a blitzed London street. The whole experience is well laid out and presented, and is worth the average twenty-minute wait for your tour. The main customers tend to be school parties, so, for a shorter waiting time, try traditional dinner breaks. Before leaving the museum be sure to visit the well-stocked bookshop. Here an extensive range of publications is available, as well as the recommended double CD British War Broadcasting 1938-45. The nearest tube station to the museum is Lambeth North on the Bakerloo line.

The RAF Museum Hendon

With free entrance, open between 10.00 and 17.30, this vast collection of aviation memorabilia requires a full day to do it justice as it traces the history of the RAF from its origins to the present day. It houses a huge collection of aircraft including many from the Second World War. If you have limited time, however, head for the Battle of Britain Memorial Hall where the entire block deals with the events of 1940-1941. Inside, you are transported back in time by a number of talking dioramas, including a London street scene. There is a sizeable collection of Civil Defence apparatus on show before you emerge into a small seating area. Here, with the ingenious use of projectors and lighting, a short film explores the cause and effect of the Battle of Britain and the bombing of London, using contemporary images and newsreels. It is not to be missed. When the curtain rises, you can walk among the aircraft, many of them German, and get as close as possible to Heinkels, Junkers 88 and Messerschmitts, thus completing your visit.

Again there is a well-stocked souvenir and bookshop, especially noted for its stock of back-issue *After the Battle* magazines. To get to Hendon on public transport from central London try the Thameslink station at Mill Hill Broadway or Colindale Underground Station which is on the Northern Line; alternately, Bus no 303 stops right outside the museum.

INDEX